Frank McGuinness

PLAYS TWO

Frank McGuinness was born in Buncrana, Co. Donegal,
and now lives in Dublin and lectures in English at
University College, Dublin. His plays include: *The
Factory Girls* (Abbey Theatre, Dublin, 1982), *Baglady*
(Abbey Theatre, Dublin, 1985), *Observe the Sons of
Ulster Marching Towards the Somme* (Abbey, 1985;
Hampstead Theatre, London, 1986), *Innocence* (Gate
Theatre, Dublin, 1986), *Carthaginians* (Abbey, 1988;
Hampstead, 1989), *Mary and Lizzie* (RSC, 1989),
The Bread Man (Gate, 1991), *Someone Who'll Watch
Over Me* (Hampstead, West End and Broadway, 1992),
The Bird Sanctuary (Abbey, 1992), *Mutabilitie* (RNT,
1997) and *Dolly West's Kitchen* (Abbey, 1999; Old Vic,
2000). His translations include Ibsen's *Rosmersholm*
(RNT, 1987), Lorca's *Yerma* (Abbey, 1987), *Peer Gynt*
(Gate, 1988; RSC and international tour, 1994; RNT,
2000), Chekhov's *Three Sisters* (Gate and Royal Court,
1990), Brecht's *The Threepenny Opera* (Gate, 1991),
Hedda Gabler (Roundabout Theatre, Broadway, 1994),
Uncle Vanya (Field Day Production, 1995), *A Doll's
House* (Playhouse Theatre, Broadway, 1997), *The
Caucasian Chalk Circle* (RNT, 1997), Sophocles's *Electra*
(Chichester, Donmar, Broadway, 1998), Ostrovsky's *The
Storm* (Almeida, 1998) and *Miss Julie* (West End, 2000).

by the same author

Plays
DOLLY WEST'S KITCHEN
MARY AND LIZZIE
SOMEONE WHO'LL WATCH OVER ME
MUTABILITIE
OBSERVE THE SONS OF ULSTER MARCHING TOWARDS THE SOMME

FRANK MCGUINNESS PLAYS ONE
(*The Factory Girls, Observe the Sons of Ulster Marching
towards the Somme, Innocence, Carthaginians, Baglady*)

Translations
A DOLL'S HOUSE (Henrik Ibsen)
PEER GYNT (Henrik Ibsen)
ELECTRA (Sophocles)
THE STORM (Alexander Ostrovsky)
MISS JULIE/THE STRONGER (Strindberg)

Screenplays
Brian Friel's DANCING AT LUGHNASA

THE DAZZLING DARK: NEW IRISH PLAYS
(edited by Frank McGuinness)

FRANK McGUINNESS

Plays Two

Mary and Lizzie
Someone Who'll Watch Over Me
Dolly West's Kitchen
The Bird Sanctuary

Introduced
by the author

faber and faber

This collection first published in 2002 by Faber and Faber Limited
3 Queen Square London WC1N 3AU
Published in the United States by Faber and Faber Inc.
an affiliate of Farrar, Straus and Giroux LLC, New York

Typeset by Country Setting, Kingsdown, Kent CT14 8ES
Printed in England by Mackays of Chatham plc, Chatham, Kent

For Philip

Contents

Introduction, ix

Mary and Lizzie, 1

Someone Who'll Watch Over Me, 77

Dolly West's Kitchen, 171

The Bird Sanctuary, 265

Introduction

Returning to past plays is strange. It's like going back to places you lived in and thought you'd never leave. You do, for the same places grow up, as it were, and move away. On meeting them again, it might be bad manners to remark on how they have changed.

The excellent Irish novelist Molly Keane always admired beautiful manners. In her best novel she identified them as Good Behaviour. At their hearts' core these plays centre around rituals and the need to disrupt ritual. Mary and Lizzie Burns drink dangerous tea with Jenny and Karl Marx. The Henrysons destroy each other at family dinner. Dolly West throws her kitchen open to the world and runs the risk of emptying it. In their teetotal captivity, Edward, Michael and Adam throw a wild party, somehow knowing that it's a wake. After these engagements nothing will be the same.

Comedy thrives on change. I suppose these plays are about change. Are they comedies? When they want to be. Have they good manners? They push their luck on occasion, but don't we all? They try to know themselves from the inside out. That knowledge transforms them from what I thought they would be into what they actually became. I like to believe they have a life of their own, but then I would.

They are related, naturally, but they are independent. It's interesting to watch them repeat certain sayings, certain gestures, show signs of a shared genetics. They might stand on common ground, but they took root in territory that is their own, and no one is going to shift them. Their reception into world has been rough at times, but they are not for running. That's the way they were reared.

Frank McGuinness

MARY AND LIZZIE

For Peter Holmes
and to the loved memory of Katy Behean

Mary and Lizzie was first performed by the Royal
Shakespeare Company in The Pit at the Barbican,
London, on 27 September 1989. The cast was as follows:

Mary Burns Maureen Beattie
Lizzie Burns Lesley Sharp
A Pregnant Girl Cate Hamer
An Old Woman Pip Hinton
A Priest Nicholas Woodeson
Mother Darlene Johnson
A Pig Robert Demenger
Queen Victoria Nicholas Woodeson
Karl Marx Simon Dormandy
Frederick Engels Simon Russell Beale
Father Robert Demenger
Jenny Marx Katy Behean
A Boy Timothy Stark
Chorus Jane Cox, Caroline Harding, Maggie Carr,
     Kate Byers, Candida Gubbins, Louise Kerr

Director Sarah Pia Anderson
Designer Ultz
Lighting Geraint Pughe
Music Shaun Davy
Stage Management
     Jan Bevis Hughes, Richard Reddrop, Sarah Cox

The author acknowledges the assistance of all who
participated in the workshop on *Mary and Lizzie*,
organised by the RSC at Stratford-upon-Avon in
July 1988.

Characters

Mary Burns
Lizzie Burns, her sister
The Women in the Trees
A Pregnant Girl
An Old Woman, Mother Ireland
A Priest
Mother, to Mary and Lizzie
The Women of the Famine
A Pig
Queen Victoria
Karl Marx
Frederick Engels
Father, to Mary and Lizzie
Jenny Marx
A Boy
The Women of the Camps

One

THE CITY OF WOMEN

Lizzie They say long ago in this country there was a city of women who lived in the trees. They'd followed soldiers who they believed loved them. At the camp they were received like lepers and were banished into the forest. Fleas ate them, and they drew blood, scratching the world from themselves, weeping up the trees like withered leaves in rain.

A community of women. They live in the trees. They sing.

Women
Sén trua nach mise, nach mise,
Sén trua nach mise Bean Phaidín.
Sén trua nach mise, nach mise,
Sén trua nach mise Bean Phaidín.

Lizzie The next thing I knew this man was beside me.

Women How did you know?

Lizzie It wasn't his face. The next thing I knew my fingers were moving.

Women How did they move?

Lizzie They knew their way home.

Women
Sén trua, nach mise, nach mise,
Sén trua nach mise Bean Phaidín.

Lizzie The next thing I knew my fingers were bleeding.

Women How did they bleed?

9

Lizzie Red roaring red. The next thing I knew his heart was beating. How did I know? It wasn't my own. The next thing I knew his fist was inside me.

Women How did you know?

Lizzie It cut like a knife. The next thing I knew his voice was like honey.

Women How did you know?

Lizzie Sweet in my mouth.

Lizzie starts to climb the trees. The Women sing.

Women
Sén trua nach mise, nach mise,
Sén trua nach mise Bean Phaidín.

Lizzie The next thing I knew the girl, she was rising. Up to the stars and into the moon. The man he came following, following, following, with his fist raised to the sun. (*Lizzie moves from tree to tree.*)

Women Run, girl, run, run.

Mary enters on the earth. She sings low.

Mary
Sén trua nach mise, nach mise,
Sén trua nach mise Bean Phaidín.

Silence.

Lizzie Mary?

Mary Lizzie.

Lizzie How are you here?

Mary I followed you.

Lizzie Why?

Mary We've work to do away from here.

Lizzie Such as what?

Mary Wander the earth.

Lizzie Do it yourself.

Mary Where you are, I am.

Lizzie How did you find me?

Mary I heard your heart beating.

Lizzie How did you hear?

Mary It was near breaking. Will I show you your heart?

A Pregnant Girl enters. She carries a bayonet.

Pregnant Girl My name is gone, my good name.

The Women mock the girl.

First Woman My name's gone.

Second Woman Gone, gone.

Third Woman She's wearing clothes.

Fourth Woman Woman's clothes.

Fifth Woman She's a woman.

Sixth Woman My name's gone.

First Woman Strap her down.

Second Woman Strip her naked.

Third Woman Strap her.

Fourth Woman Naked, strap her naked.

Fifth Woman Strip her.

Pregnant Girl They won't let me in, they won't let me in.

Mary In where?

Pregnant Girl In at the camp, the army camp. My man said to follow his regiment. I'd find him waiting at the Curragh camp. But they won't let me in. They gave me this weapon. (*Raises the bayonet.*) They sent me here, bag and baggage, they won't let me in.

Mary How far are you gone?

The women whistle.

Women How far are you gone? How far are you gone?

Lizzie Are you lonely down there, Mary?

First Woman Can you climb a tree?

Second Woman Leave her behind you.

Third Woman The one carrying death.

Fourth Woman When it dies, she'll rise among us.

Fifth Woman Do you see us in heaven?

Sixth Woman Will you stand with the saints?

First Woman The saints on the cross.

Mary Lizzie.

Second Woman Who is she?

Lizzie My sister.

Third Woman No such thing here.

Fourth Woman Only wind, rain and water.

Fifth Woman Smell of sight and smell of sound.

Sixth Woman Waiting here for a good hiding.

First Woman But at least it's the touch of a man. Get the one carrying a bastard.

The Women tumble to the earth. They surround the Pregnant Girl. They threaten her with the bayonet. All the time they howl the word 'run'. The bayonet suddenly falls. The Pregnant Girl is still. The Women separate about her in silence. The First Woman starts to weep. She raises both her hands.

Where are my hands?

Second Woman You cut them off to send to your soldier.

Third Woman So he could find his touch upon you.

The First Woman shows her tongue.

First Woman Where is my tongue?

Fourth Woman You bit to its root and spat it from you.

Fifth Woman The last words of love would be to your man.

First Woman Where are the legs that walked after him?

Sixth Woman You took an axe and chopped them off you.

First Woman Here I would stay until he returned.

Pregnant Girl Where is he?

First Woman Where yours is.

Pregnant Girl How long have you waited?

First Woman How old is the earth? It must be ancient. Old as the hills. He never returned. Tell her our story. All the one story. Tell her.

Lizzie Who?

First Woman You, Lizzie Burns. Who still has a name. You'll lose it, like we lost ours, so speak, before it's lost.

Lizzie (*sings*)
    I courted a soldier who loved another,
    Neither father nor mother, sister nor brother,
    For love it is lonely, looks for no shelter,
    Content in itself, though inclined to wander.

    The soldier went walking through lands barren
    And followed the road of the sparrow and wren.
    In trees I searched for him, through leaves hidden,
    For my love he chased the hare from its den.

    My love when he left me promised me jewels,
    Bracelets and bangles and soft silver bells,
    But love it is lonely, inclined to be cruel,
    The gem that it gives is the burning swell.

    And soldiers go walking through lands barren
    And follow the road of the sparrow and wren.
    In trees we search for them, through leaves hidden,
    For my love he chased the hare from its den.

Silence.

Pregnant Girl Have you ever killed anything?

First Woman A bird. A young one. I laid the egg. I smashed it against the wall. Wrung its neck with a cord. Left it in the trees, lamenting. Curse that carcass from you.

Mary Burns lifts the bayonet.

Mary Or carry it. (*She turns it towards herself.*) Carry your burden until it's time to cut it from you, let it fly. (*She plunges it into her body. She removes it, unbloodied.*) If it's alive, it's only yourself.

She is unmarked.

First Woman I saw you kill –

Mary Nothing.

First Woman You killed –

Mary I killed nothing. You killed nothing.

First Woman A child. It was mine, red. A man took me.

Mary You gave your body.

First Woman My body?

Mary Your body. You gave your body.

First Woman No such thing. Nothing. Get you and your sister and your name out of where none of you belong. You are a dead woman.

Mary So are you.

> *Mary holds out her hands to Lizzie. Lizzie shakes her head. Mary withdraws her hands. Lizzie walks to her. The Pregnant Girl sits crouched, nursing the bayonet. Mary and Lizzie kiss. The Women in the trees vanish.*

Lizzie Kiss and tell.

Two

THE EARTH OPENS

Mary and Lizzie walk back and forth.

Lizzie They say long ago in this world there were two women, Mary and Lizzie Burns. Why were they in this world? To wander it. Wander through time, through place, for that was their way, their story. This is the telling of Mary and Lizzie, and the ways they walked through lives together.

An Old Woman enters, singing.

Old Woman
 Fill, fill a rún Ó,
 Fill, a rún Ó, is na imigh uaim,
 Fill ort a chuid de'n saol mhór
 No chár fhéiceann tú nglóir mur bfilleodh tú.

 Turn, return, my grace, my stór,
 Turn, my own, do not leave me,
 Turn, return, to heaven's door,
 See me, my son, do not grieve me.

 You've betrayed Peter, you've betrayed Paul,
 Betrayed priest and pope for gold,
 The keys of the kingdom you've let fall,
 Turn to me, son, before the grave cold.

 Turn, return, my grace, my stór,
 Turn, my own, do not leave me,
 Turn, return, to heaven's door,
 See me, my son, do not grieve me.

The Old Woman stops singing.

Old Woman This land's mine. What's mine is yours.

Mary We don't want land.

Old Woman I'm worth my weight in gold and silver.

Lizzie We want neither.

Old Woman Then what can I give you? Do you like men?

Mary Yes.

Old Woman Do you have faith in men?

Lizzie Yes.

Old Woman I had a son who was beautiful.

Mary Kind?

Lizzie Good?

Old Woman Are you hungry?

Lizzie Yes.

Old Woman Shall I feed you?

Lizzie What with?

Old Woman A song for your throat.

Lizzie The hunger's here. (*Lizzie touches her belly.*)

Old Woman Have you known a man?

  Silence.

What's a man to you?

Lizzie Strong.

Mary A song.

Old Woman I choose you for my son.

Mary Choose both or neither.

Old Woman Better be both, for my son's lost. Lost the keys of the kingdom. He's betrayed Peter and Paul. Betrayed priest and pope. Commit the sin of lust with my beautiful son. Follow me to him.

Mary Where is he?

The Old Woman produces a golden key.

Old Woman Locked in the house this key opens. He converted from Catholic to Protestant. I close my eyes when I see him now. Sin with my son. Then he'll seek his penance. Before a holy priest. Heaven's door he's slammed shut in his face and the gates of Hell stand open before him. Follow me.

Mary Not until I know which direction. Where's the door this key opens?

On the earth the Old Woman makes the sign of the cross with the key. She places the key in the centre of the imaginary cross. The earth opens.

Lizzie It's a grave.

The Old Woman shakes her head.

She's the devil.

The Old Woman laughs.

Don't go with her.

Old Woman She'll come.

Lizzie No.

Old Woman She'll love my beautiful son.

The Old Woman climbs into the earth.

Mary Maybe it's home, Lizzie.

Lizzie In a grave?

Mary It's only the earth.

Lizzie I'm afraid of the grave. It's where I was born. Our mother died when she gave me birth. Mary, what did she look like?

Mary Come and see.

Mary and Lizzie enter the earth.

Three

THE MAGICAL PRIEST

Priest Praise be to Christ who is King of the waters, mighty and wonderful in earth and water. Lead me, Aquinas, who doth walk in love and knowledge. Hear me, great Luther, in faith's defence. Shelter me, Calvin, in fate and fortitude. A mighty tower let me construct, an alphabet of God, ye prophets of Revelations. Let me recite for my people a service of splendour that they shall eat the fruits of love, of good and evil. For my hand and my mouth shall speak such truths that they who witness shall feel their breath turn to fire. And from this divine service I shall exclude my mother.

Turn, turn, ye Catholic damned, fear, fear for the error of your ways, fear as I feared for my many errors. I gave this body to the whore of Babylon, robed in the regalia of Catholic priests. I wear this raiment as penance and punishment. I saw the light that is Satan's throne. Children of Ireland, have you seen Satan? Children of Ireland, have you seen my mother? Do not listen to her lies and scandals. I am no Catholic, no Protestant. I worship both faiths with new eyes.

Shall I spell out the faith of the future? Christ is amongst us with a new commandment. Hate one another as I have hated you. Jesus it was who tempted Satan, promised him the throne of Rome. Satan agreed on one condition. Amend the commandments of the Lord. In this island I preach new religion. Where there is God, take his name in vain. Remember thou keep the Sabbath savage. Kill the honour of father and mother. Steal neighbour's wife and neighbour's goods. Convert, convert and covet, covet.

Enter Old Woman.

Wash ye in waters of revelation, dance in the beauty of virgins' blood.

Old Woman Jesus, Mary and St Joseph.

Priest Fear not the dawn of holy salvation, embrace the night of your new soul.

Old Woman Have you been reading that unfortunate Bible?

Priest Christ is amongst us, the beast and the beauty, come to his house and covet conversion.

Old Woman Cursed be the day I came across this.

Priest You wouldn't have if you hadn't been spying.

Old Woman I was right to watch you like a hawk.

Priest A singularly appropriate bird of prey, Mother. Pray? No sense of humour, Catholics.

Old Woman Have I lived to see one of mine turn?

Priest Yes, you have, Mother dear. Turn from blind faith to a wise one. I have been Catholic, I have been Protestant, now I am both and wish you were too.

Old Woman Never.

Priest Please yourself. But I sent you on business. Did you fetch me a cobweb?

Mary and Lizzie enter.

Old Woman Here are two spiders, son.

Priest Mother, they are women.

Old Woman Fine women.

Priest I've noticed. You've wasted your time coming here. I'm spoken for. It's time Mother Ireland accepted that. The amount of girls she's encouraged to climb through the earth – astonishing really. I take it she has informed you of her mystical plan? She finds a nice girl, I fuck her, fall into despair over broken vows of chastity, return to the Catholics, abandon Protestantism, do my penance and forget my allegiance to the religion I've founded? Then all's well, yes? No go, Mother dear. Not interested. Would you excuse me, I've to say Mass. Black Mass, that is.

Old Woman My son died and this was put in his place.

Priest She's mad.

Old Woman Love him.

Mary Why?

Priest Yes, why, Mother?

Old Woman He needs a woman.

Mary He needs a wife.

Priest I like her. She has brains. They'll be delicious fried in a little butter. We eat them in our religious sacrifices, the handmaidens who climb down here. Good hunting, Mother. (*Points at Lizzie.*) A leg will do nicely, and a little slice of lung.

Lizzie I won't be eaten.

Priest Don't be difficult. Tears distress me. I know they're necessary. We collect them, you know. I pour them into a chalice and offer them up as a gift to my God from the poor of the Irish people, who will always be with us. Silly saying really, not one of your best, Jesus, it only encourages the buggers.

Lizzie If I were to convert –

Priest To my strange religion, which is the destiny of Ireland? A killing combination of two defunct faiths that can only survive by feeding off each other? Forgive me, I'm getting carried away by my vision of the future. You were saying?

Lizzie If I were to convert, would you still kill me?

Priest Yes, lucky you. Straight ascent to Heaven. No questions asked. So do convert, my dear – what is your name, child?

Lizzie Lizzie Burns.

Priest Charming.

Lizzie When I was twelve I saw the Devil.

Priest What was he like?

Lizzie It was a she.

Priest What was she like?

Lizzie points to Mary.

Lizzie Her.

Mary Say the Black Mass.

Priest Why?

Mary In my honour.

Priest I can't. I'm no longer a priest.

Old Woman Once a priest, always a priest, my beautiful son.

Mary Yes, he is beautiful. Shall we marry him?

Lizzie Shall we eat him?

Priest Mother, do something.

Mary His lungs and kidneys.

Priest They belong to God. I belong to God.

Lizzie His legs and arms.

Priest God's terribly possessive.

Mary His feet.

Lizzie His hair.

Mary His heart.

Lizzie His eyes.

Mary His soul.

Lizzie Yes, his soul.

Mary He's signed away his soul.

Lizzie Let's eat his soul.

Priest You'll have to find it first.

Mary It's in my pocket.

Lizzie It's up my skirt.

Mary Between the two of us.

Priest Mother.

Old Woman Good girls, keep going.

Mary Bite us and draw blood.

Lizzie We're poor lost Catholics.

Mary We want to convert.

Lizzie Convert you, body and soul.

Priest O Jesus.

Mary Your sweet Protestant soul.

Lizzie Your strong Catholic body.

Priest Why did you bring them here?

Lizzie We came of our own accord, Mary and Lizzie.

Priest Would you like a Bible?

Mary We can't read.

Lizzie We don't want to.

Mary We want to get married.

Priest Then do, do.

Old Woman They want to marry you, pet.

Priest I'm married to myself.

Old Woman And you never said?

Priest It came as quite a shock to me.

Old Woman When did this happen?

Priest The day I converted. I was Catholic and Protestant. I'm a mixed marriage, Mother.

Old Woman And you see where it's led you?

Priest Yes.

Old Woman You broke my heart. Why?

Priest It's a mystery, Mother.

Old Woman No more mysteries. No more marriages.

Mary Marry me.

Priest Who to?

Mary Myself.

Lizzie Marry me.

Priest Who to?

Lizzie My mother.

Priest I don't have the words to either ceremony.

Mary Make them up as you go along.

Priest Do you, Mary Burns, take this woman, Mary Burns, to be your lawful wedded wife?

Mary I do.

Priest To have and to hold, in sickness and in health, till death do you part?

Mary I do.

Priest I now pronounce you woman and wife. And do you, Lizzie Burns, take your mother as your lawful wedded wife?

Silence.

Well?

Lizzie I want to see her.

Priest Beyond my power.

The Priest and the Old Woman fade.

Lizzie She's dead. She's in the grave. And we're in the earth. We can meet here. Show me her. Mother.

Mary She'll come.

Lizzie Why?

Mary You've called her.

Lizzie What did she look like?

Mary Look.

Four

THE FEAST OF FAMINE

There is baroque music. The Mother is attended by six women in elaborate, jewelled costume. The women carry six covered gold platters. At the click of the Mother's fingers, the music ceases. The Mother stares at Mary and Lizzie.

Mother Yous pick your time to call, what do yous want? I'm watching over you morning, noon and night but of course that's not enough. Oh no, the old horse here can't get a minute's peace. What are you looking at with them sheep's eyes?

Lizzie Is it you?

Mother As far as I know. Look at the cut of them, shame a body. Do something with your hair. Like comb it. Two bales of hay. If I had lived to rear you, you wouldn't be out like that. Nothing I can do now. You're old enough and ugly enough to know better.

Lizzie We're not ugly.

Mother Listen to that. Better fit for you to offer your dead mother a chair. Never mind, I'll stay on my feet.

Lizzie I'll find you a chair.

Mother I don't want a chair.

Lizzie Do you want a chair?

Mother I said I didn't.

Lizzie She wants a chair.

Mother You couldn't like that one if you'd just given birth to her.

Lizzie You gave birth to me.

Mother I know, I died. I was tired. And I couldn't watch you die. You might have. Two others did.

Lizzie Mary lived.

Mother Mary was Mary.

Lizzie Who was I?

Mother The last born. It does funny things to a woman, birth. You choose your time to live and die. When you arrived, I chose to go. I let you live. I gave you my life. Don't bother thanking me. I wanted out of this world. Heaven's great, girls, best of everything. Are yous married yet?

Mary No.

Mother Don't. And don't have children. They kill you. Look at these, God love them. (*Points to the Women.*) Every one, died at childbirth.

Lizzie How?

Mother They could see the future. When I had you last, I saw my future – one daughter after another until the end of my time. I'd had enough, so I closed my two eyes. Same with them. But they saw more than their own death coming. It's bad news for this country. I want yous out of it. Go to England now.

Lizzie We can't speak English.

Mother What in God's name do you think you're talking in?

Lizzie Gaelic.

Mother Dead as a duck. Forget it. I've arranged for you to be given the gift of tongues. I want no thanks. Think of it as a Christening present. You were beautiful when you were born. So was Mary. So were the dead ones. Ah well, no point lamenting.

Lizzie I love you.

Mother Are you looking for something?

Lizzie Nothing.

Mother Just as well. That's what's in store for you here. If you stay.

Lizzie I want to stay.

Mother Well, if you won't listen to me, maybe you'll listen to strangers, then. Tell them what's coming to poor old Ireland.

First Woman Famine.

Second Woman Death.

Third Woman Disease.

Fourth Woman Exile.

Fifth Woman Hunger.

Sixth Woman Fever.

Mother The girls are a bit on the gloomy side, but they know what they're talking about. Show them. Listen, have you eaten? Here's the feast of famine. Music for the feast.

> *A slow lament begins. The First Woman lifts the platter's lid to show a stone. The Second Woman shows a book. The Third Woman shows rags. The Fourth Woman shows a spoon. The Fifth Woman shows a straw. The Sixth Woman shows a bone.*

The Pregnant Girl enters, carrying a cauldron and a bayonet. The Women sing separately.

First Woman
If this stone could speak, it would say,
Throw me in the pot, throw me in the pot.

Second Woman
If this book were read, it would write,
Throw me in the pot, throw me in the pot.

Third Woman
Were I these rags, I would ask,
Throw me in the pot, throw me in the pot.

Fourth Woman
This spoon wants a mouth to shout,
Throw me in the pot, throw me in the pot.

Fifth Woman
I lay on straw and heard it sigh,
Throw me in the pot, throw me in the pot.

Sixth Woman
My child shrank from skin to bone,
Throw me in the pot, throw me in the pot.

During the song, the Pregnant Girl has collected the objects into her cauldron. She stirs the ingredients with the bayonet. The Women sing.

Women
When it's dead, boil its head,
Make it into soup and bread.
When it's dead, boil its head,
Make it into soup and bread.

First Woman
Soup of stone and bread of straw,
Eat the rat, the field, the haw.

Second Woman
    Bread of bone and bread of rags,
    Eat the dead of starving hags.

Third Woman
    Head of stone and empty spoon,
    Eat the stars and belly's wound.

The Women sing.

Women
    Do this all of you in memory
    Of the race hunger freed.
    Do this all of you in memory
    Of the race that ate its seed.
    Do this all of you in memory
    Of the race that died in need.

Fourth Woman
    Here the roadside, here the cabin,
    Here the dying, dying millions.

Fifth Woman
    Here the fever, here the din
    Of the dying, dying millions.

Sixth Woman
    Here the hands stretched in pain
    From the dying, dying millions.

From the cauldron the Pregnant Girl takes out
potatoes. She cuts them with the bayonet.

Mother It will fail, the potato crop, girls. There'll be
famine. It will spread through the land. There will be
neither warning nor consolation. Blight will fall from sky
to soil. A million dead. A million gone to foreign lands.
Get you now to your father. England is no promised
land. But they look after their own. You'll have the bite

in your stomach. Leave here before the earth devours its young and old.

> *The Mother sings. The Pregnant Girl stirs the cauldron. As the Mother sings, the Pregnant Girl serves her cauldron to the Women, who drink emptiness from it.*

Soup of stone and bread of straw,
Eat the rat, the field, the haw.
Bread of bone and head of rags,
Eat the dead of starving hags.
Head of stone and empty spoon,
Eat the stars and belly's wound.
Remember feast, remember famine,
Famine feast and feast of famine.
Times of want, times of plenty,
The gentleman who pays the rent,
The gentleman who pays the rent.

> *The music turns into a reel. A Pig appears, dressed as a Victorian gentleman. The Pig dances with the Mother. The Women look on, beating time with the lid of the platters.*

Pig Tell them who I am, good woman.

Mother A pig.

Pig A special pig.

Mother A dancing pig.

Pig A speaking pig.

Mother A gentleman pig.

Pig Ladies, I have not made my introductions. Forgive me. (*Bows.*) In Ireland I am called the gentleman who pays the rent. And so I am well treated. I'm not for eating, I'm for exporting. Have you heard of landlords?

Well, I line their pockets. But pigs are of passing interest
to you humans. Self, self, self, that's all you think about.
I'll never understand you. We're born to die, but you
keep asking, Why am I here, why am I here? By the way,
why am I here?

Mother It's the feast of famine.

Pig Ah yes, famine. Terrible. Strange thing is, we animals
saw it coming, but would you believe our signs? I myself
composed a little verse or two on the whole tragic topic,
but unfortunately I was shipped off to the Saxon shores
before publication were possible. I threw it into a passing
cargo ship, you know, the ones with rotten flour so
generously bestowed for famine relief, but I'm sure no
one found it and the poem is lost for ever.

Mother Have you forgotten it?

Pig I remember every word.

Mother Tell us.

Pig (*clears his throat, and recites*)
  In the most distressing country that ever has been seen,
  Lived a lovely little family, we shall call the family
    Green,
  They had a little cabin and a little bit of land,
  And they worked and worked it until they could
    barely stand.
  They lived on spuds and buttermilk and a little bit
    of fish,
  And the rest of what they grew made the landlord's
    dainty dish.
  They had children who had children who had children
    with child,
  And the children of these children grew exceedingly
    wild.

And to curb this population the Good Lord sent
  a plague,
They grew thinner and thinner in arm and in leg.

In the most distressing country that ever has been seen
Died a lovely little family, they all had turned quite
  green,
For a great big butcher came along holding up a knife,
And they screamed for mercy, they screamed for dear
  life.

We'll call the butcher empire and the knife we'll call
  its greed,
And it cut the throat of Ireland, leaving it to bleed.
But what care for the Irish, aren't they dirty pigs?
Leave them in their squalor to dance their Irish jigs.
Wash your hands and wash your hands and wash
  hands again
Of the blood and the fever and leave no sign of stain.

Good friends and true friends, listen to my tale,
Here for you's a moral that never fails,
God protects the rich and the rich protect themselves,
The poor can go hang and the Irish go to Hell.

*The Pig bows. The Pregnant Girl approaches him.
She slits his throat with the bayonet. The Pig squeals
in horror and runs off. The Pregnant Girl approaches
Mary and Lizzie.*

Mary What are you carrying in your belly?

Pregnant Girl A stone to build my house.

She hands Mary the stone.

Lizzie What's in the house?

Pregnant Girl A book to say I live there.

She hands Lizzie the book.

Mary How will you live?

Pregnant Girl In rags and in want.

She hands Mary the rags.

Lizzie What will you want?

Pregnant Girl A spoon to stir my sorrow.

She hands Lizzie the spoon.

Mary What is your sorrow?

Pregnant Girl A straw in wind.

She hands Mary the straw.

Mary What will the wind carry?

Pregnant Girl The bone of a child.

*She hands Mary the bone. She raises the cauldron and
the bayonet.*

I'll hold on to these. Value what you're given. They'll be
useful one day.

Lizzie What for?

Pregnant Girl That would be telling.

Lizzie Tell.

Pregnant Girl Look what happens to those that tell.
They get their throats cut.

*The Pregnant Girl and the Women fade. Mary and
Lizzie are left alone with their Mother.*

Mother So.

Mary So.

Mother Well.

Lizzie Well.

Mother Your father's in a place called Manchester. Go to him there.

Mary Why will the famine be let happen?

Silence.

Mother Anyway, yous better go.

Lizzie How will we get there?

Mother Swim.

Lizzie I'm afraid of water.

Mother Jesus, two grown women and I still have to do everything for them. Swim.

The Mother licks her hand. She touches the foreheads of Mary and Lizzie. Lights fade. Music.

Five

PASSING THE TIME WITH THE QUEEN OF ENGLAND

Lizzie So this is England? Who will we meet here?

Mary Whoever's in store for us.

Lizzie Who do you want to meet?

Mary Time for a man.

Lizzie You, a man? (*Laughs.*) You're half man already, Mary.

Mary How?

Lizzie You could always do a man's work.

Mary It's only work.

Lizzie You'd enjoy a man.

Mary Would he enjoy me? I think I'd be jealous of him enjoying me. I wouldn't like to be jealous. But I'd like a man. Before I'm ancient. Jesus, age, wouldn't it break your heart?

Lizzie Will your heart break?

Mary Only when I hear it.

Lizzie Breaking?

Mary Beating. What's the difference?

Lizzie Poor old Mary, she'll die of love.

Mary Poor old Mary, she'll die of loneliness.

Lizzie What about the man?

Mary He's still to be found.

A young woman, Queen Victoria, enters. She sees Mary and Lizzie and screams.

Lizzie Jesus, girl, take it easy.

Mary Take it easy, take it easy.

Victoria Do you mean me any harm?

Lizzie No, pet, you're safe enough here.

Mary Are you being followed?

Victoria Of course, morning, noon and night, they hound me.

Lizzie Who?

Victoria My people.

Lizzie Your family don't trust you?

Victoria Family? No, my people. They insist I rule. And I'm too young.

Mary Rule where?

Victoria Are you being amusing? England. I am Queen Victoria, and I wish to die.

Lizzie Who's Queen Victoria?

Victoria Me. Don't be overawed. A simple curtsey will suffice.

Mary How do you want to die?

Victoria Drowning.

Mary Well, you're dressed for it.

Victoria I always am. State occasions demand it. God, I'm knackered by state occasions. Still, England demands,

England demands, England demands . . . too much.
A cruel mother, this country. Pushing, watching, pushing,
all the time. England.

Lizzie What's it like, England?

Victoria Aren't you English?

Mary We've just come from the water.

Victoria Good gracious, are you mermaids? Where are
your tails? (*She sniggers.*)

Lizzie Watch your fucking mouth, lady.

Victoria You wouldn't talk to me like that if Lord
Melbourne were here.

Mary He's not.

Lizzie What put a man into your head?

Victoria There's nothing between us. I am not an adultress.
I swear it before God and man. (*Throws herself on her
knees.*) I am a good, clean, respectable girl, saving herself
for marriage. There is nothing between me and my Prime
Minister. He could be a woman for all I care. Tittle-tattle,
tittle-tattle.

Mary Tittle-tattle.

Lizzie Tittle-tattle.

Victoria You don't believe me?

Mary We do.

Lizzie Millions don't.

Mary But we do.

Lizzie You're the talk of the town.

Mary Down under the ocean.

Lizzie Young mermaids aren't allowed to mention your name.

Mary Blush at the sound of it.

Lizzie Tails grow quite red.

Mary Shocking to fish and fin.

Lizzie You count for nothing down there, girl.

Victoria Nothing?

Lizzie Nothing.

Victoria You mean if I were to leap into the sea and sink to the bottom of your kingdom – you have a king, I take it?

Mary No.

Victoria Down to your . . . your republic – hateful word – I would be –

Mary Ignored.

Victoria Oh. So it's only on the earth I command respect? Well then, that settles it. I'd better gobble up a lot more of it than this sceptred isle, this seat of Mars, this teeming womb of kings. Methinks I am a prophet, newly blessed. I will see the lands of England swirl before me like a skirt, lifting me and my people through the continents of the earth. Which part of my expanding empire would you mermaids wish to conquer?

Lizzie Manchester.

Victoria Why?

Lizzie Do you know it?

Victoria I've smelt it.

Lizzie What's it like?

Victoria Words rarely fail me. They do not on this occasion. An open sewer, Manchester.

Lizzie We're searching for our father.

Victoria I know what you mean.

Lizzie Our mother's dead.

Victoria The poor have all the luck.

Mary What will you do?

Victoria I'm born to rule. My destiny, England's destiny, decreed by God, by fate and by me. A myth I am, but not yet a monster. There will be wonderful stories about my terrible life. As a child, they dressed me in black. It was in preparation. Not for being queen, but for being a woman. What is England like? Go and find out. I can tell you one thing. It isn't content. So it roams the world, looking for contentment. And finds it nowhere. For no one wants it. That's a secret between me and the empire. Put it under your hat, when you can afford one. I worry for poor England when the wandering's over. Where will it go then but into itself, and what will it find? A tenement. The England that was wont to conquer others now makes a conquest of itself. Some third-rate isle lost among her seas. How shall we cope? By lying, I suppose. Methinks I am a prophet newly blessed. The old order changeth, yielding place to the new. Find it. Find it in Manchester. Would you excuse me? I must rule. I have an empire to govern. May as well enjoy it while it lasts. I send best wishes to your kingdom under the sea. We must exchange ambassadors. I'll speak to Lord Melbourne. (*Moves to exit.*) Forgive me.

Mary Why?

Victoria I don't know. I felt like asking. Forgive me. (*She exits.*)

Lizzie Rare bird, her.

Mary She'll get over it. To Manchester.

Six

BED

Engels You know something, Karl?

Marx continues writing.

Yours is the first circumcised cock I've ever seen.

Marx What has brought my . . . penis . . . into your conversation?

Engels Well, for two men, and you'd agree on this, Karl, two men so much into materialism, it seems to me like a waste of good skin.

Marx Frederick, at the time it happened I had not as yet evolved my political theories.

Engels laughs.

Is this some kind of joke?

Engels Yes.

Marx I am not amused.

Silence.

Engels What are you doing?

Marx Writing a poem.

Engels To your wife?

Silence.

To a friend like me?

Marx In a way. It is for the benefit of all mankind.

Engels What's it about?

Marx A profound experience of my own. My conversion to the materialist conception of history.

Engels That should be good. What do you call it?

Marx It doesn't have a title.

Engels That's bloody daft. Poem needs a title, part of a poem, title. Stupid bloody poem, no title. I don't like it already.

Marx Why do you want a title?

Engels I like to know where I stand. Could I run a business unless it had a name? Ermen and Engels, Number 2, South Gate, Deansgate, Manchester. Textile Manufacturers. Jesus, Karl, you want to change the world and you can't be trusted to give your poem a title.

Marx Sometimes I think you are quite mad.

Silence.

Engels I'm sorry. I apologise.

Marx I accept.

Silence.

Engels Read the poem.

Marx To please you, I shall call it 'Ode to Materialism'.

Engels I like that.

Marx Thank you.

Engels Read it.

Marx 'Material powers of production, I salute you.'

Silence.

Engels Is that it?

Marx Yes.

Engels It's very good. Very unlike you. Concise. To the point. 'Material powers of production, I salute you.' Keep going. How about, 'The bourgeois relations of production are the last antagonistic form of the social process of production – antagonistic not in the sense of individual antagonism but of one arising from conditions surrounding the life of individuals in society'?

Marx That doesn't rhyme.

Engels No, it wouldn't, you see. It's only one line. The next line could be something like, 'At the same time the productive forces developing in the womb of bourgeois society create the material conditions for the solution of that antagonism. This social formation constitutes therefore the closing chapter of the prehistoric stage of human society.'

Marx Perhaps we should stick to prose.

Engels No, no, I'm off on this poetry lark. We end every line with the word society to underline man as social being. Get it?

Marx Go to sleep, Engels.

Engels Are you afraid of the dark?

Marx No.

Engels I am.

Marx Why?

Engels Dreaming.

Marx Why are you afraid of dreaming?

Engels It might come true, the dream.

Marx I don't understand you.

Engels You do. You know the way you walk for miles through somewhere you know, but you see nothing, for you're lost inside your own head? I do that. I'm lost. I'm lonely. In a funny way it's why I love the poor. I think they're lonely too. Do you love the poor?

Marx I hate them. I hate your sentimental waffle about them. I hate their ignorance. I hate their cruelty. I hate their stupidity. I hate their patience. I hate you for loving them. I hate you for drinking with them, laughing with them. I hate the poor.

Engels Lightens the load, a good laugh.

Marx The load is not to be lightened. Not to be lifted. The load's there to be carried. The poor are beasts of burden. I won't ease the burden, but the beasts can be released on civilisation, and when they are freed, they will shake the world to its very foundations. So the poor are lonely? No, no one is lonely, no one. Tired, broken, despairing, destroyed, yes, but not lonely. There's no such thing as loneliness. Or at least there won't be, in our future.

Engels Are you sure?

Marx Are you not?

Engels Yes. (*Cuddles up to Marx.*) Do you know 'The Sleeping Beauty'?

Marx Why?

Engels My favourite.

Marx It's a girls' story.

Engels Suppose it is.

Marx I'm going to sleep.

Engels You know, I like girls' stories. I like girls. I should find a girl.

Marx A witch.

Engels What?

Marx A wicked witch. Like mine.

Engels Jenny?

Silence.

Are you asleep? I'm afraid of the dark. Demons, dragons, but not witches, funniy enough.

Silence.

Not very rational, is it? If you were awake, you'd laugh me out of it. No, you'd argue me out of it. Just like my father. Arguing. It was my mother who laughed. Father, always arguing. Father. That's why I'm afraid of ghosts. Spectres. Haunting me.

Marx rises and sleepwalks. Engels sings low.

It is the dead of night,
The house is full,
My father's in the house,
He eyes my mother.

Rather her than us,
Rather her than us.
Haunts me to my grave,
To my grave, haunted.

Rather her than us,
He eyes my mother,
Father in the house,
Haunts me to the grave.

Silence. Marx moves to exit.

Where are you walking in your sleep, Karl? Back to your wife?

Marx exits.

I'd like to kill my father. I wouldn't call it murder. I'd call it war. You would approve of that. I like approval. I'll send you money, Karl. It's his for the taking. My father's, that is. I'm afraid of my father, even if he's dead and gone. He haunts me through Germany, through France and England. He haunts the whole of Europe. A ghost, a spectre. There may be no escape. For him, as well as me. Night night, Father. Night night, Karl. Night night, Europe. Night, night night.

Seven

MANCHESTER

Light changes. Mary and Lizzie enter. Music. Engels sees them.

Mary Are you afraid of the night?

Lizzie Are you afraid to dream?

Mary Do you see in your dreams?

Lizzie Will you see with us?

Engels Who are you?

Lizzie Will you walk with us?

Mary Through Manchester?

Lizzie Can we ask our father?

Mary He works in Manchester.

Lizzie Will you hold his hand?

Mary Will you walk with us?

Lizzie Through Manchester?

Mary Will we show you Manchester?

Lizzie The poor of Manchester?

Mary Will we show you our father?

Lizzie Will you hear our father?

Engels Who are you?

Mary Witches.

Lizzie Poor women.

Mary Are you lonely?

Lizzie Are you rich?

Mary Do you live in a palace?

Lizzie In a mansion?

Mary Is it your father's mansion?

Lizzie Our father lived there.

Mary In your palace.

Lizzie In your factory.

Mary Come with us.

Lizzie Meet our father.

Mary Mister Engels of Manchester.

Industrial sounds pierce. Half-naked, dyed brown, Michael Burns, father to Mary and Lizzie, walks. As the noise stops, the Father begins to shake. He speaks to his hands, sinking to his knees.

Father Will you stop shaking? You're the tools of my trade. Steady yourself, will you? Do you want us to starve? Body, will you have wit? What kind of humour's in you? Will you turn me blue with want? Is there anyone listening? Is there one to hear me? Body, stop shaking? Will you lead me to the workhouse?

(*Sings.*)
Fingers to the bone, fingers to the bone,
Walk through shite on your way back home.
Skies shite rain, rain shites on all,
Mouth to feed, hunger on the wall.
Army on its stomach, poor like night,
Marching, marching, brown as shite.

Women in this town, breasts laced with milk,
Men in this town, dry enough to drink.
Them in this town churn that milk to butter,
Sell it back with salt to milking mother.
Sweat from your brow earns the daily bread,
Bread black as sweat, dyed body red.

Silence.

Is there one out there?

Engels holds out his hand.

Is anyone listening?

*Engels begins to raise his hand. Father begins to rise
from the ground.*

Is there one to hear me?

Father is now on his feet. Engels looks at his hand.

Engels (*sings*)
Kill the scavengers that fly,
Above the streets of Manchester,
Owl and kite that guide their cries
Throughout the streets of Manchester,
Devouring pain red as meat,
Raw on the streets of Manchester.

Father (*sings*)
Kill the bird, the pain, the sheet
That winds the streets of Manchester.
Into profit, loss and gain,
The shroud of streets of Manchester.

Engels (*sings*)
The factory that bears my name
Opens the streets of Manchester,
Lead me through the lasting shame
That moves through streets of Manchester.

Mary (*sings*)
  Body, build the factory brown
  That made the streets of Manchester.

Lizzie (*sings*)
  Body, tear the factory down,
  Deface the streets of Manchester.

The Father looks at his hands. They shake violently.

Father Press. Press. Watch the wheel, the rope's
slackening. Press, girl, press. Watch the room. For
warmth, for wet. If the thread snaps, the machine stops.
Never let the machine stop. Never let the hand stop.
Press, woman, press. Watch the thread winding. For
Christ's sake, watch the thread winding. Man is his
machine, woman's work is never done. Keep your eyes
peeled to the thread. Wind your eyes out from your
body. Man's body's woman's work. Sore eyes, sore
hand, sore work, sore body. I want to work, I want to
die, I need to wash the dirt off myself. I need to die.

The Father fades.

Engels Are you afraid of the dark?

Mary No.

Lizzie No.

Engels Will you live with me?

Mary Together.

Lizzie Together.

Engels Are you afraid of changing the whole wide world?

Mary We've met the man.

Lizzie Kind.

Mary Good.

Lizzie Then the match is made, till death do us part.

Mary Sisters in life.

Lizzie Sisters in love.

Engels Living with Frederick Engels.

Engels stands between Mary and Lizzie. They link arms. They walk back and forth.

Lizzie Years ago in this country they say two women met a man and they went walking through Manchester. The women gave the man safe passage through the dangerous poor, for he believed in changing the workings of the world, and because they loved this world, they believed in him. They showed him the poor and they showed him their father and they showed their race and themselves to him, the two women, Mary and Lizzie Burns, sisters in life, sisters in love, living with Frederick Engels, for they believed in the end of the world. Listen to the world changing. Listen to the world ending.

They look at each other.

Eight

DINNER WITH KARL AND JENNY

Mary and Lizzie have equipped themselves with fans.

Marx The value form, whose fully developed shape is the money form –

Mary Money?

Marx Yes. It is very elementary and simple.

Mary Simple.

Marx Yes. Nevertheless the human mind –

Lizzie Mind?

Mary Human?

Marx Yes. The human mind has for more than two thousand years sought in vain to get to the bottom of it, while on the other hand –

Lizzie Hand?

Mary The other.

Lizzie Yes.

Marx To the successful analysis of much more composite and complex forms there has been an approximation –

Lizzie Why?

Marx Because the body –

Mary The body?

Lizzie I like the body.

54

Mary Yes.

Marx – as an organic whole –

Lizzie Legs.

Marx – is easier to study –

Mary Tits.

Marx – than are the cells of that body.

Mary Body.

Lizzie Legs.

Mary Tits.

Lizzie Frederick's more of a tits man than a leg man.
Which are you, Karl?

Silence.

Marx In the analysis of economic forms, moreover,
neither microscopes nor chemical reagents are of use.

Engels I don't mind a bit of leg as well, Lizzie.

Marx The force of abstraction must replace both.

Mary Abstraction?

Marx But in bourgeois society –

Mary rapidly interrupts.

Mary The commodity form of the product of labour
on the value form of the commodity is the economic cell
form. To the superficial observer the analysis of these
forms seems to turn upon minutiae. It does in fact deal
with minutiae. But they are of the same order as those
dealt with in microscopic anatomy, and you can quote
me on that one, Karl.

Marx You are in fact quoting me.

Mary Aren't you the intimidating, smart boy?

Marx If I bore you ladies, my wife –

Lizzie Are you married?

Marx You know I am.

Mary I'd love to be married.

Lizzie So would I, but he won't have us. You shame us, Frederick, you're a disgrace.

Mary No, he's a man of principle. He has no wife.

Lizzie Karl has.

Mary Well, he would.

Lizzie I like his wife.

Mary So does he.

Lizzie So does everybody.

Mary Karl had better be careful. Our bourgeoisie, not content with having the wives and daughters of the proletarians at their disposal, not to speak of common prostitutes –

Lizzie Stop, I feel faint.

Mary – take the greatest pleasure in seducing each other's wives.

Lizzie Are you worried about her and Frederick?

Mary Nah, she has no tits.

Lizzie She has legs.

Mary Have you ever seen them? One night I looked up her skirt. There was a gap between the ground and her knees.

Lizzie Poor Jenny.

Marx These women are not welcome in my house.

Engels I think they know, Karl.

Marx Then why do you insist on bringing them?

Engels They insist on coming.

Lizzie We wouldn't miss it.

Mary We're respectable women, visiting friends.

Lizzie Having dinner.

Mary Dinner with Karl and Jenny.

Lizzie Lovely.

Mary Not really. We bought it.

Silence.

Marx I have frequently acknowledged my friend's financial assistance.

Mary Then why do you look at his women with poison in your face?

Marx You are not his women, you are his whores.

Lizzie So are you.

Mary So we're equal. All equal. All respectable. Tell your wife.

Lizzie Where is she?

Marx Indisposed.

Silence.

Her nerves.

Silence.

57

Every day she wishes she were in the grave. She has grown old. I can no longer cope with her complaining. No, not complaining. Her fantasies.

Mary Can she cope with yours?

Marx I have no fantasies.

Mary No, you have philosophies. Good philosophers, the two of you. Bright as buttons. Brains to burn. Tell me your philosophy, Frederick.

Engels Mary, you're being cruel and stupid.

Mary Cruel, yes, you sometimes deserve it, but stupid, never, you wouldn't let me, so tell me your philosophy.

Engels For you to mock?

Mary For me to hear.

Engels And when you hear, have your laugh?

Mary No laugh. I'll listen. Tell me your philosophy.

Engels Division into classes has a certain historical justification. It has this only for a given period under given social conditions. It was based upon the insufficiency of production.

Mary begins to open Engels's fly.

It will be swept away by the complete development of modern productive forces.

Lizzie goes behind Engels and strokes his hair. His fly is now undone.

Engels What the hell are you doing?

Mary Listening.

Lizzie Go on.

Engels And in fact the abolition of classes in society presupposes a degree of historical evolution at which the existence –

Mary Existence.

Mary's mouth moves towards Engels's fly. Lizzie kisses his forehead.

Engels – not simply of this or that ruling class, but of any ruling class at all –

Lizzie You like being ruled sometimes. You love it.

Marx My God.

Engels begins to grow agitated.

Engels Class distinction itself has become an anachronism.

Lizzie Hold a grip on yourself, man.

Engels Intellectual leadership –

Lizzie slaps Engels's face.

Lizzie Don't rush, take it easy.

Engels – by a particular class of society has become not only superfluously but economically –

Lizzie Politically – intellectually –

Engels – a hindrance to development. (*Engels reaches climax. He roars.*) That point has now been reached.

Lizzie kisses Engels. Mary holds both in her arms. They kiss Mary. Lizzie climbs on Engels's shoulders. Mary gets herself between his legs. Engels howls with pleasure.
Jenny enters, carrying a tea tray. On the tray are a dish of strawberries, a vase of flowers and two sheets of paper.

Jenny Tea?

Engels Excuse us, Jenny. I was just illustrating to the company the distinction between utopian and scientific socialism.

Lizzie I'm utopian; she's scientific.

Mary and Lizzie release themselves from Engels.

Jenny Really? Would you care for a strawberry?

Marx We were expecting dinner, my love.

Jenny There will be no dinner, my sweet.

Marx Why not, my angel?

Jenny You don't believe in angels, my lamb.

Marx I believe in you, my swan.

Jenny Thank you, my deer.

Marx Where is dinner, my spaniel?

Jenny There is no food, my ox.

Marx Why not, my owl?

Jenny We have no money, my camel.

Marx Frederick provided us with money, my sick lioness.

Jenny I burned it, my hawk.

Marx Why?

Jenny It was given to me by a tainted hand.

Mary Mine.

Jenny By a tainted mind.

Mary Mine.

Jenny I do not like you in my house.

Mary I don't like you in your house.

Jenny You gentlemen see fit to entertain these women. How different we are as a species, male, female and those between both. Excuse me, I will adjourn to my room –

Mary And go mad.

Silence.

Jenny You cunt.

Mary You cunt.

Lizzie Three cunts.

Silence.

Engels Tea?

Mary lifts the vase of flowers. She removes the flowers from the vase. She drinks the water from the vase. She throws the flowers at Jenny's feet.

Jenny Thank you.

Mary and Lizzie bow to Jenny. Jenny bows back. She walks to Marx with the tray. He takes the tray from her.

Offer our guests food, husband. I apologise for the poverty of the fare, but the dish is beautiful. I like to look at it. It convinces me I am a wealthy woman.

They each take a strawberry and eat.

As a young woman, I was quite pretty. Do eat more strawberries, they're quite delicious. Forgive my nerves. I bought the strawberries all by myself. Are you proud of me, Karl? Karl has lived with my nerves so long he scarcely notices them. I drive him out of the house. He is a good man, I've made him what he is today. We love each other. For him I would pawn my life. Which is just as well. It is the only thing we have not pawned yet.

(*Laughs.*) My strength is I find it all so funny. Karl Marx
cannot feed his family; his wife and mainstay cannot
help her husband. Aren't we silly-billies? I do encourage
him now with the odd extravagant gesture. That is why
I burned the money. Have you ever watched money
burning? A piece of paper, turning to ash. I was conducting
a scientific experiment. Will it burn to gold? It didn't,
Karl. Ash to ash and dust to dust, money is death, my
love, and you have been dealing in death for so long,
my darling, I have lost direction and you are losing
control, for the house is falling about our ears and now
I only hear you speak to me in the crumbling walls
and squeaking doors and the holes in the roof and your
bloody books. I would like to put a match to your books
and watch them blaze like an old boot and say, This is
my life and if life be a wheel, I am spinning out of
control. You cannot help me, husband. Help me. Help
me. I am a noble woman. I am wife to Karl Marx, who
cannot feed his family but who would feed all mankind.
It's a conspiracy against me. You and your whores, Mr
Engels, conspire with the world against me. I do realise
what is going on around me.

Silence.

Eat. Eat the strawberries. I picked them myself.

*Jenny squeezes strawberries in her hands until they are
red.*

When I was young and could look in the mirror, I once
saw myself like a tree, and then one night I lit a candle
and Karl appeared. I got such a shock. I thought it was
my husband, he took my breath away. Perhaps he didn't.
We've travelled together through life. To where, I don't
know. Do eat these strawberries. To death, I suppose.
I picked them myself. (*Looks at her hands.*) I have a
mind of my own. Fetch me the tray, Karl.

Marx goes to her with the tray. Jenny takes the sheets of paper and wipes her hands with them.

Read my hands. What's written on the paper. Handwriting. Only I can read your handwriting. Shall I whisper a sinister prophecy of coming catastrophe?

Jenny whispers, reading from the crumpled paper.

All fixed, fast-frozen relations with their train of ancient and venerable prejudices and opinions are swept away, all new-formed ones become antiquated before they can ossify. All that is solid melts into air, all that is holy is profaned, and man is at last compelled to face with sober senses his real contradictions of life and his relations with his kind.

Silence.

Well, are you proud of your wife? Did you believe she'd think that up? I wrote that, not you, my love. Isn't this my handwriting?

Marx turns from her.

Solids melting into air, my husband. Holy, now profaned, our life. His sober senses recoil from me. Face me, face your kind. Am I your contradiction? Are we not speaking? My husband and I are in opposition tonight. I am afraid he will brand me revolutionary. Well, it is high time revolutionaries should openly, in the face of the whole world, publish their views, their aims, their tendencies, and meet this nursery tale –

Marx grabs the paper from her.

Marx A nursery tale is right. You reduce me and my work to your handwriting. You are ridiculous, Jenny –

Jenny No, I am redundant. A useless piece of production, past child-bearing, and there were no sons –

Marx I love my daughters.

Jenny There were no sons. When you're silent, I can read your lips. They curse me in Hebrew. I can read your mind. Every word you've written, I've thought before you.

Marx That is lying. That is fantasy.

Jenny takes out notes of money.

Jenny Is this? I didn't burn it. There I was lying. But I will if you don't help me. (*Drops a note.*) Pick it up. (*Drops another note.*) Pick it up. (*Drops another note.*) Pick it up.

Marx collects the money.

My husband understands money. It grows on the tree. You are so kind, Frederick. I love you for your cruel kindness. I find you so funny. My husband finds you useful. Do you girls find him useful or funny? Do you love him for his money? You know how money talks. Have you heard how he talks about you? Have you seen what he's written?

Mary We don't read.

Jenny Shall I tell you what he's said?

Lizzie He's never mentioned our name.

Jenny He's named your race, however. Do you think he loves you? Listen to *The Condition of the Working Class*. This extract is so amusing. 'Drink is the only thing which makes the Irishman's life worth living. His crudity which places him but little above the savage, his filth and poverty, all favour drunkenness. The temptation is great, he cannot resist it, and so when he has money he gets rid of it down his throat.' (*Laughs loudly.*) Forgive me, it is so amusing. You would agree there is some truth in it.

Don't you find it funny? Shall I read on? 'With such
a competitor the English working man has to struggle,
with a competitor on the lowest plane possible in a
civilised country, who for this reason requires less wages
than any other. All such as demand little or no skill are
open to the Irish. For work which requires long training
or regular, pertinacious application, the dissolute,
unsteady, drunken Irishman is on too low a plane.'

Lizzie Read on.

Jenny I can't, you don't find it funny.

Mary (*sings*)
    My young love said to me, my father won't mind,
    And my mother won't slight you for your lack of kine,
    And she moved away from me and this she did say,
    It won't be long, love, until our wedding day.

Lizzie (*sings*)
    The people were saying, no two were e'er wed,
    But one had a sorrow that never was said,
    And she moved away from me with one star awake,
    Like a swan in the evening moves over the lake.

Mary Read on.

Jenny 'When, in almost every city, a fifth or a quarter of
the workers are Irish, or children of Irish parents, who
have grown up amid Irish filth, no one can wonder if the
life, habits, intelligence, moral status – in short the whole
character of the working class – assimilates a great part
of the Irish characteristics.

Mary *and* **Lizzie** (*sing*)
    Last night she came to me, my dead love crept in,
    She crept in so softly, her feet made no din.
    As she moved away from me, these words she did say,
    It will not be long, love, until our wedding day.

Mary (*sings alone*)
   Last night she came to me, my dead love, my dead love.

   Silence.

Engels You know it's the truth.

   Silence.

You know what you showed me.

Mary Mo ghrá thú, Iá da bhfacha thú.

Lizzie I loved, the day I saw you.

Marx You're dangerous, a rotting mass, sitting there, passive, the lowest of the low, you might have your uses, you could be swept into life, but in your condition you're part and parcel of the old regime.

Lizzie And you offer us a bun, we lick the sugar but throw away the bread, is that it?

Mary We'd fail you, yes?

Marx Yes.

Mary As you've failed us?

Engels I've never failed.

Mary You have failed me.

Engels I have never failed.

Mary What's the fear in you?

Engels Fear?

Mary Us? Our like? Is that behind it all? You don't know us. You fear us. So you'll remove us. The breast-beaters would save our souls for the sake of their own salvation. How will you save us? Change the world, eh? Mr Engels is afraid of the dark. We're the dark.

We're the night. Will I show you the dark? Will I lead you through the night to come?

Engels Have you lost your reason?

Mary It's dead, reason.

Jenny Dead love.

Marx It's begun to live.

Lizzie Dead as a doornail.

Jenny Dead.

Marx On the contrary it shall open doors and it shall knock down palaces, the doors of prisons. In the prisons of the mind we shall construct the palaces of freedom –

Jenny I should like to see this night to come.

Mary gives Jenny a stone.

Mary Worn like a stone, here is your charm. Fade.

Jenny fades. Mary gives Marx a straw.

Name be broken, sacred, profaned, scatter throughout the wide earth. Fade.

Marx fades. Mary gives Engels the book wrapped in rags.

Through you be I remembered, live when I die. Fade.

Engels fades. Lizzie stirs the air with the spoon.

Lizzie Who are we calling?

Mary Whoever comes.

Lizzie What will we give them?

Mary What they give us.

Lizzie What if it's nothing?

Mary Then so be it.

Lizzie How do we get there?

Mary Making a wish.

Lizzie With what?

Mary A human bone. (*Mary raises the bone.*) Let us enter the night to come.

The Pregnant Girl enters.

Pregnant Girl Shall I show you the night? Shall I show you your heart? I heard your heart breaking.

Nine

WHERE

A boy enters. He speaks in Russian.

Boy *Вы нас видите?*

Pregnant Girl Can you see us? Yes, I can.

Boy *Вы можете это описать?*

Pregnant Girl Can you describe this? Yes, I can.

Boy *Вы помните утро и ночь?*

Pregnant Girl Do you remember morning and night? That's when they came, morning and night.

Boy *Это когда они пришли, утром и ночью, вошли в дверь, посмотрели на мою маму.*

Pregnant Girl Came through the door, looked at my mother.

Boy *Моя мама хочет попить воды.*

Pregnant Girl My mother would like a drink of water.

Boy *Она головой ударяется об пол, степи России.*

Pregnant Girl Her head hits the floor, the steppes of Russia.

Boy *Она плачет за всю Россию.*

Pregnant Girl She is crying through the whole of Russia.

Boy *Они застрелили моего отц, его надо похоронить.*

Pregnant Girl They've shot my father, he has to be buried.

Boy *У моей мамы кровь течёт, я должен её найти.*

Pregnant Girl My mother's bleeding, I have to find her.

The Boy speaks in English.

Lizzie Where will we find your mother?

Boy Where there are women walking.

Lizzie Where will we find your father?

Boy Inside my mother.

Mary What will we tell them?

Boy Listen.

The Boy weeps.

Mary Why do you look at me like that?

Lizzie Where are we?

The Boy fades. Mary stands in silence.

Mary?

Silence.

What are you hearing?

Silence.

What are you seeing?

Mary Women walking.

The Women of the Camps enter. They sing in chorus.

Chorus
 Comb not your hair,
 Wash not your face,
 Earth through your hair,
 Earth on your face,
 Take ye and eat,

Body and blood,
Love's left the earth,
Froze human hearts.

The Pregnant Girl hits the cauldron with the bayonet.

First Woman
Have you seen my son,
Wandering the forest?
I found my son's blood
On the leaves of the forest.
How was it his?
I was told by the forest.
I told the earth
Of crimes in the forest.
They locked me away,
But I see the forest.

Chorus
Take ye and eat,
Body and blood,
Love's left the earth,
Froze human hearts.

The Pregnant Girl hits the cauldron with the bayonet.
The Second, Third and Fourth Women sing in chorus.

Second, Third *and* Fourth Women
I wrote down my name,
Lest it be forgotten.
I hid it in the earth,
Let it be forgotten.
I burned it in fire,
May it be forgotten.
I drowned it in water,
It was not forgotten,
For air told the earth,
Water's not forgotten.

71

They locked me from air,
But fire's not forgotten.

All the Women sing in chorus.

Chorus
Take ye and eat,
Body and blood,
Love's heard the earth,
Healed human hearts.

The Pregnant Girl beats the cauldron with the bayonet.
The Fifth and Sixth Women sing.

Fifth *and* Sixth Women
I dreamt of my death,
My crime was to dream.
I dreamt of my birth,
I entered my dream.
I woke from my death,
It was their dream.
They crushed my head,
My brain went to dream.
They locked me in sleep,
But I'm still my dream.

Chorus
Take ye and eat,
Body and blood,
Love's heard the earth,
Healed human hearts.
Take ye and eat,
Body and blood,
Love heard the earth,
Healed human hearts.

The Women exit. The Pregnant Girl beats wildly on
the cauldron with the bayonet. She stops suddenly.

Pregnant Girl Too long I've carried this burden inside me. Time to be free.

The Pregnant Girl gently cuts her belly open with the bayonet. She begins to laugh low. From inside her she takes a wooden box. She opens the lid. It is empty. She lets the box fall into the cauldron. She laughs.

At long last, I've buried my death.

The Pregnant Girl holds out her hands to Mary and Lizzie.

Pregnant Girl Give me back what I gave you.

Lizzie We gave it away.

Pregnant Girl Everything?

Lizzie hands her the spoon.

You?

Mary looks at the bone. She puts it in her mouth. It chokes her. She spits it into her hand.

Give it to me, that's not your job.

Mary What is my job?

Silence.

Will I never give birth?

Silence.

Will I always be haunted? Will I always be lonely?

Silence.

Tell me.

The Pregnant Girl takes the bone and places it in the spoon. She puts bone and spoon in her belly.

73

Pregnant Girl Start again, I suppose. Rough life, eh? No rest, no rest, until the grave. But there's no grave either. Just the earth. Wander it. It is too lonely.

The Pregnant Girl leaves Mary and Lizzie. Silence.

Mary Is anyone listening?

Silence.

Is there one to hear me?

Silence.

Frederick, when I call, will you not come to me?

Silence.

Are you not there? I have something to tell you. I remember you. And you will be remembered, because you loved the earth and loved me, little knowing either. I will be remembered by a line in your life. Frederick Engels lived with two Irishwomen, Mary and Lizzie Burns. Little does that tell. Little do they know. Little did we know. You'll fail, but you'll be forgiven, for you loved, and love forgives. Forgive? Love forgets. Forget Frederick. Forget Karl. Forget Jenny. Forget Lizzie. Forget Mary. Their hearts were human, beating, and I hear mine, breaking. The heart, Jesus, the human heart, beating, breaking.

Lizzie Mary.

Mary Leave me.

Silence.

Leave me.

Silence.

Leave me.

Lizzie leaves Mary. Mary looks about her. She closes her eyes. She bows her head. Strange light fills the stage. The Mother appears. She opens Mary's eyes.

Mother Why are you here?

Mary I died, Ma.

Mother What from?

Mary Heart.

Mother Pity about you.

Mary Pity.

Mother I suppose you're looking for something. You wouldn't be here if you weren't.

Mary What am I going to do?

Mother You can't come in here. I've just cleaned it. You're going back to life. I'll come with you for the laugh. Don't argue with me. I miss the earth. Where's Lizzie?

Mary She's still alive.

Mother That's handy. Now how do we get back?

Mary I don't know.

Mother Shut your mouth. I'm thinking. Sing to me.

Mary Why?

Mother That's how the earth became. That's what I learned here. God didn't make the earth. We sang it. He heard us and joined in. We did it together, creation. There's no difference between God and man, or woman for that matter. Isn't that interesting? Will we head home? Do you want to see me create the earth?

The Mother sings. As she sings, Mary walks arm-in-arm with her.

When Lagan streams sing lullabies,
There grows a lily fair.

Mary (*sings*)
The twilight gleam is in her eyes,
The moon is in her hair.

Mary *and* **Mother** (*sing together*)
Then like a lovesick leanashaí,
She has my heart on fire.
No rest have I nor liberty,
For love is lord of all.

Lizzie appears. She joins in the song. The three walk, linked, about the stage.

Mary, Lizzie *and* **Mother**
No rest have I, nor liberty,
For love is lord of all.

Mother Well, so be it.

Lizzie Aye, so be it.

Mary So be it.

SOMEONE WHO'LL WATCH OVER ME

Do Bhrian Fear Cróga

Introduction

by Brian Keenan

I have on many occasions been invited to Frank McGuinness's play *Someone Who'll Watch Over Me*. For whatever reason, it was not until last Monday evening that I could afford myself the opportunity.

I had spoken to Frank some months after my home-coming. He told me of his proposed work and with much sympathy, great anxiety and tender fearfulness, he said he would do nothing further if I felt it caused any danger or hurt to those men who at that time remained in chains in Lebanon. I asked him simply to explain what he had in mind. I was intrigued as he spoke. I watched him lay his ideas before me. Here was a man writing in the dark, but somewhere in his imagination he had found bright sparks of illumination.

Though he had no information on which to base his play, I could see he had the touchstones of emotional truth. I simply answered him: 'Go for it, Frank', realising that what-ever the reality was I had no right to abort his poignant foetus. To deny a man or his work is no man's right. Frank McGuinness had shown me and my still imprisoned friends a massive courtesy and sympathy. I could only return it.

On Monday evening I sat in the Abbey unnoticed and watched something that had become strangely more than oneself. It was a curious experience. During my captivity I had often sat and watched myself. That, too, was a curious experience. Frank's play could only be fiction. I knew the man. Could I divorce myself from the reality?

The opening – shallow lights on a man chained and lean-ing on a radiator – choked me in its immediacy. Like see-ing an old photograph and instantly recalling unwanted

81

memories I sat frozen, but with a part of me melting. Can expectation be such a frozen thing?

Then, with a pace and ferocity I had not expected, the play and its people blasted out of the shadows. A life-enhancing interaction of human souls becomes a substantial and fleshy thing. Frank McGuinness, with his words and imaginative power, walked into a place where 'angels fear to tread' and came out dazzling. From that beginning I knew this was to be an uproarious celebration.

The man had caught human frailty and worshipped it; to err is indeed delightfully human. It reveals us to ourselves and Frank McGuinness's mirror was not faulted. There were more than a few moments when I choked back intense realisation. With uncanny intuitive force *Someone Who'll Watch Over Me* touched wellsprings that moved the drama out from its vague topicality and sang to Everyman.

With painful emotional force Edward says to Adam: 'Let me be able to do my worst to you, and you to me . . .' Thus began a burning in a rich linguistic fire that seared and scorched the audience with a laughter that was at times born out of pain as much as humour. It was obvious that Frank wrote this work with a terrible panic and a sore heart. All too often he hit those moments which Joyce called his 'epiphanies'. The bright sparks of starlight in black sky which was the constant backdrop to the drama could not have been more exact.

In these star-bright moments McGuinness hit on, with a playwright's subtlety, guilt, love, loneliness and all the gamut of emotions that make us, break us and remake us. But these lights of illumination probe our darkness. He questions, for example, if the empowerment and loss of language can overcome absolute loss – when nothing is left but the flesh on our bones and perhaps a chain with which to rattle meaning.

Many things struck me. At times I gagged back tears, hoping no one would hear, and then thought about the marvellous theatricality of the play. The letters home which each of the men speaks to the others were a fabulous vehicle. In their fabrication they lie and love ambiguously but they reveal more than their words convey.

The same dramatic mechanism is employed with the 'make a movie' sequences. Adam, Edward and Michael each adopt and play out a persona. Their movies are a screen through which they re-invent themselves and the nothingness of their world. Which of us has not played that game? And how many of us know its value?

In Scene Two McGuinness tries to pull together and resolve his drama. The ringing message is that brave men are only so when they conceive the female in themselves. Each man speaks often of his father. The father image is a hovering shadow, but in phrases like 'possessed by my father', McGuinness hints at the female echoing in us all.

I loved dearly *The Song of Songs*. I don't know where Frank got that from. It was a moment from my own captivity. Its eroticism is one of the most loving gifts to the world. I knew it, as obviously did the author, who used it with a poignant force. Again there was the unseen seam of the feminine sewing the parts together.

What more can I say? Frank McGuinness's play made me choke and cry and laugh and hold myself. When a man of mighty talent takes on a daunting enterprise he is either, as we say in Belfast, 'a bollocks or a big man! . . .' Thank you, Frank, for bringing me home again. You have a four-square set of shoulders, an imaginative sensitivity matched only by craftsmanship. I hope someone will watch over you, too!

Someone Who'll Watch Over Me was first performed at the Hampstead Theatre, London, on 10 July 1992. The cast was as follows:

Michael Alec McCowen
Adam Hugh Quarshie
Edward Stephen Rea

Director Robin Lefevre
Designer Robin Don
Lighting Designer Nick Chelton
Artistic Director for the Hampstead Theatre Jenny Topper

The play was subsequently produced in New York by Noel Pearson at the Booth Theatre, Broadway, in November 1992.

Characters

Michael
Adam
Edward

Setting
A cell

Time
Now

PROLOGUE

*In darkness Adam's voice is heard humming lowly,
'Someone to Watch Over Me'. His voice grows slightly
louder as light slowly rises.*

*He stops singing. The light now just about picks out
his shape.*

SCENE ONE

*Complete light. Ella Fitzgerald sings 'Someone to Watch
Over Me'.*

*Edward and Adam are together in the cell. They are
separately chained to the walls. Edward is centre stage;
Adam is stage right. The chains are of sufficient length
to allow freedom of movement for both men to exercise.*

*Edward is dressed in a loose blue T-shirt and white
football shorts. Adam is dressed in black T-shirt and grey
shorts.*

*They exercise in silence. Adam's exercises are rigorous;
Edward moves through his paces more sluggishly.*

Edward That was Ella Fitzgerald singing, 'Someone to
Watch Over Me'.

Adam What was?

Edward My eighth and final record for *Desert Island
Discs*. It is also my single choice of record. Good old
Ella. Did you have *Desert Island Discs* in America?

Adam No. What is it?

Edward You pick eight records and your favourite among the eight. Then you choose a luxury. Then a book, apart from the Bible and Shakespeare. They're already on the desert island. My book is a guide to home-brewing beer, and my luxury is a beer-making kit. And Ella Fitzgerald would sing to me. I'd be happy on a desert island. Easy pleased, that's me. An easy-going man.

Silence.

Jesus, the boredom, the boredom, the bloody boredom. And they're coming up the hill at Cheltenham and Dawn Run is fading, she is fading, the great Irish mare will not complete the unique double of the Cheltenham Hurdle and the Gold Cup, she's tiring and she jumps the fence, she's gaining strength in the air, she's wearing them down, she passes one, she passes two, a third she passes and the winning post's in sight, she's done it, she's won. Dawn Run for Ireland, mighty woman. She's won the Gold Cup.

Silence.

Jesus, it was a real pity I didn't have money riding on her. Dawn Run. Did I ever tell you about Dawn Run?

Adam She was your favourite horse. She won both her great races. She was magnificent. You loved her and would have married her, but it couldn't have worked out. She was a horse and you were human. Besides, she was Protestant, you were Catholic, and you were already married. You've told me about Dawn Run.

Edward Sarcastic Yankee. She was a hero, that horse.

Adam So were Glasgow Celtic when they won the European Cup, and I don't want to hear about them, either.

Silence. Adam exercises strenuously.

How many press-ups did you do?

Edward Didn't count.

Adam How many?

Edward Twenty.

Adam You did not.

Edward Fifteen.

Adam You did not.

Edward Twelve.

Adam Eleven. One more than yesterday.

Edward Yes.

Adam Come on, Edward, we've got to keep going. I got to get you into condition. You know that, you agreed to it. We can have competitions when you're in condition.

Edward I don't care about competitions or about my condition.

  Silence.

Adam Yeah, yeah, I know what you mean. Who am I fooling? Who the hell am I fooling? Me. That's who. No, no brooding. No blaming myself. That way I go under. I will not go under.

  Silence.

Edward The boredom, the boredom, Jesus, the boredom.

  Silence.

I'm going to start to brood.

Adam I will not brood.

Edward I'm going to start to blame myself.

Adam Don't.

91

Edward I'm imagining where I would be, if I hadn't come to this country.

Adam Where would you be if you hadn't come here?

Edward At home wondering what it would be like to be here.

Adam Yeah.

Edward laughs.

Edward 'There's some that cannot stay at home, and our Eddie, he is one of them.' My father's words, proved right, proved right. Time and time again. He has to be the big man, this boy, never getting stale, never being safe. And look where he's landed today. Far across the sea. Not in Amerikay nor even in Australia, but in the land of the fucking Lebanon. Jesus, could I have found it on the map before I came here? I leave one kip at home to come to this kip here – oh Christ, look at this place. The dirt of it. Chained to a wall. No women. Food's fit for pigs. You don't know if it's morning or night. You don't know who belonging to you is alive or dead. You can't even go to the shithouse without one of them handcuffed to you, watching your very bowels move. The heat, the dust, the smell. It's a bad hole. But I will say one thing. It's better than being in Strabane.

Adam What's wrong with Strabane?

Edward If you ever want proof there's no God, go to Strabane. Hell on a stick, sweet Strabane. It's not as bad as Omagh. Omagh, Omagh, God protect us all from Omagh. Omagh has a cathedral and a hospital in it. The hospital is slightly more reminiscent of Chartres. I screwed this woman in Omagh one night. When I looked at her in the sober light of morning, I thought she was a man.

Adam Were you married at the time you screwed with her?

Edward Don't remember. Why do you ask?

Adam Making conversation.

Edward You're making judgements.

Adam I don't make judgements.

Edward No, you just listen. Let me ramble on, you store it all up, then you size it up. Well, after two months sizing it up, what kind of specimen do you make of me? What kind of childhood would you say I had?

Adam Remarkably happy, I'd guess. You don't mention your mother. That's unusual. Something else is unusual. You barely talk about your own kids.

Edward Barely.

Adam Why?

Silence.

After two months, can't you tell me?

Edward I don't know them. Working too hard, playing too hard, me. Like father, like son in that respect. I didn't know him until it was too late. I don't know them. Now I never will. Because we're going to be in here for a long time. They could be grown men and women by the time I next see them. If I next see them.

Adam You're an Irishman. You're from a neutral country. They'll let you go.

Edward Didn't I think that? Wasn't it me waving the green passport in their faces, roaring, 'Ireland, Ireland'? They still stuck the gun up my arse and dragged me in here. Green passport, neutral country? What's that to these boys? Save your breath, Adam. We'll be old men before we're out of here. We're stuck here.

Silence.

We're stuck here.

Adam begins to exercise again.

For the love of God, will you give it a rest? Do yous Americans ever stand still?

Adam Would you prefer I were an Arab?

Edward I don't go for Arabs that much. The sand blows up their skirts and they're not allowed to scratch themselves. The itch has them the way they are, excitable.

Adam You're pretty excitable yourself today.

Edward And you never are?

Adam I don't take it out on you if I am.

Edward You should. It might give me something to fight against.

Adam I dislike fighting.

Edward Do you really dislike it? I thought the fighting was our business, in our own ways. I report it, you – what do you do about the fighting? When we were covering the Northern bother, the boys we really hated were the Italians. I remember why. Their big interest was in photographing kids. Kids crying, kids cut to pieces, preferably dead kids.

Adam I am not interested in dead kids. I am not a photographer.

Edward No, you're – what? Someone that makes the fighting all nice and clean and scientific. You stand back and examine the effects of war on innocent young minds.

How very kind, doctor. Disturbed young minds. You want them disturbed, don't you, doctor? Research, publish, profit, as I said. Make your money. Like myself, Adam. Doing a job. Very professional, Adam. Very profitable. Very American.

Adam You piece of shit.

Edward Money, Adam, you were in it for the money.

Adam And what the hell were you in it for? By your own dirty admission –

Edward It was my dirty admission. I say I came here for the money. You don't, but you did. So, who's the piece of shit? You are.

Adam I want to crack your fucking face open. I'm going to fucking kill you. If I've to listen to you much longer, I will kill you.

Edward You can't, Adam. Even if you could, you haven't got that in you.

Adam Shut up.

Edward You're not a killer. Isn't that a good thing, doctor?

Adam They haven't broken me yet.

Edward The Arabs? No, but I've broken you, Adam. Haven't I?

Adam Nearly. Why?

Edward About time, I've broken you. You think you've all the answers. You don't. I got through to something in you that you don't have an answer for. Whatever that cool head is hiding, I do not know, but I do know that cool's going to crack, it has to, and we'd better both be prepared for when it does. Whatever else about this place, we're in it together, we have to stick it out together. We'll come out of this alive. One favour – let me be able to do my worst to you, and you be able to do your worst to me. Is that agreed? That way, as you say, they won't break us, for we'll be too used to fighting for our lives.

Adam Will we get out alive?

Silence.

I do get scared. I miss my home.

Edward That's all I wanted to hear you say.

Adam I've said it. All right?

Edward One step nearer home, saying it.

Adam Ed, don't break me. Don't let me go mad. Say you want to go home as well.

Silence.

Edward I want to go home.

Adam Say it again.

Edward I want to go home.

Adam It's all right, Edward.

Edward I want my wife.

Adam She's all right.

Edward My kids, I want to see them.

Adam You will.

Edward My wife, my kids, please, let me see them. God, please. Let me talk to them. Let me go home.

Adam No.

Edward I want to go home. Arabs, Arabs –

Adam No.

Silence.

Edward We're going mad.

Adam We're in Lebanon.

Edward Yes.

Adam I'm in Lebanon.

Edward So am I.

Edward sings 'Someone to Watch Over Me'. His voice fades as the music of the song plays. Lights fade.

SCENE TWO

The music of the song continues to play as the light rises.
Michael has joined them in the cell. He too is bare-footed, wearing a white T-shirt and black shorts. He is chained to the wall, stage left.
Michael sleeps. Adam reads the Bible, the Koran sits open beside it. Edward lies slumped, watching Michael.

Edward Still no sign of life out of the new boy. How long do you think he'll be conked out for?

Adam He should be awake soon.

Edward Poor bollocks. He's in for a bit of a shock if he expects daylight. He must be out cold for the best part of twelve hours. Yeah, I'd say he'd soon come to.

Adam Yeah, he should.

Edward A bit of new company would liven the place up. I hope he speaks English. Jesus, I hope this isn't the start of a rush hour as well. How many of us do you think they could stick in the one room?

Adam I don't know, Edward.

Edward At least they've left him his bottle of water. If he wakens with a thirst on him he can drown it. Drown your sorrows, boy, dry your tears. Mourning and weeping in this valley of tears.

Adam Biblical.

Edward What?

Adam Valley of tears.

Edward Is that what you're reading? The Bible?

Adam Yeah.

Edward It's nice of them to leave us the Bible and the Koran.

Adam They pass the time.

Edward For you.

Adam If you want to read either they're here for you.

Edward Not a chance. I hate religion. All religion. Bad for you.

Adam It passes the time.

Edward Religion?

Adam Reading.

Edward Why are the Irish so religious?

Adam Why?

Edward I've asked the question.

Adam I suppose because they're always thanking God.

Edward What for?

Adam That they're not Belgian.

Edward I think your man looks a bit Belgian. Maybe he's German. I hope he's not.

Silence.

The Germans and the Dutch, they're buying up the whole West of Ireland. 'No Trespassing' notices everywhere.

Silence.

It would be rough for him if he couldn't speak English.

Adam I speak German. A little German.

Edward Good for you.

Adam You find it objectionable that I speak German?

Edward A little, shitehead.

Adam I am not a shithead.

Edward I said 'shitehead', not 'shithead', shitehead.

Silence. Adam returns to reading.

Great expression that. 'Shitehead.' I like it.

Silence.

You should quit reading in this light. It'll blind your eyes.

Silence.

It's funny, you rarely see an Arab wearing glasses.

Adam They don't masturbate.

Edward How do they manage?

Adam Do you? Masturbate?

Edward Never.

Adam Nor me.

Edward Well, not before six o'clock in the morning. You have to have some morality.

Adam My record is fifteen times in one night, and I made no complaints against myself.

Edward Any Arab women?

Adam Just American girls. I like American girls.

Edward I had a fantasy about an Arab woman. She was only wearing a yashmak. I was wearing a grass skirt.

Adam Why?

Edward She was kinky. I like that. It makes a woman unique. It was a good fantasy.

Adam I like a little foreplay in mine.

Edward Foreplay? In a fantasy.

Adam Don't the Irish like foreplay?

Edward We invented foreplay. We call it drink.

Adam What turns your wife on?

Edward A bottle of vodka. What about your woman?

Adam She's Californian. She likes to imagine she's sleeping with God. This would turn her on. The Song of Songs, which is Solomon's. 'Let him kiss me with the kisses of his mouth, for thy love is better than wine . . . Whither is my beloved turned aside? My beloved's I am, and my beloved is mine . . . Make haste, my beloved, and be thou like to a roe or to a young hart upon the mountain of spices.'

Edward Not bad. I could see some women going for that.

Adam I could turn her on, then she can turn me on.

Edward How?

Adam She tells me I've a dick that could choke a donkey.

Edward Jesus, some dick.

Adam Some donkey.

Michael I'm terribly sorry, but where am I?

Edward So it's yourself, is it?

Michael Pardon?

Edward Do you not recognise me? We were at school together.

Michael I don't think so.

Edward Eton, wasn't it? Or Harrow?

Michael No, I don't – where am I?

Edward In the officers' mess, Brit Boy. A bit rough and ready, but you'll get used to it. We have. So, how's the outside world?

Michael Who are you? Why am I here?

Edward To see a movie. Maybe if you're lucky there'll be a meal afterwards.

Adam Let it rest, Edward. Are you OK, fella?

Michael is half hysterical.

Michael I simply wish to know where I am and who you are.

Edward Lower your voice, bollocks, you want us to get a hiding?

Michael I was on my way to the market and I was looking for fruit, for pears, for I had invited a few people from the university for dinner and for dessert I wanted to make a pear flan, I was walking to the market –

Edward A pear flan?

Michael For dessert. I have people invited for dinner.

Edward Then they're going to go hungry, sweetheart.

Michael Why am I chained to a wall?

Adam You've been taken hostage.

Michael Kidnapped?

Edward Yes.

Adam My name's Adam Canning. I'm an American.

Edward Edward Sheridan. Irish.

Michael I'm an Englishman.

Edward Of course you are.

Michael Who has kidnapped me?

Adam We don't know for sure.

Edward They're not terribly chatty.

Michael Why have they kidnapped me?

Edward Because you're an Englishman. How dreadfully unfair. Not cricket.

Michael Why have they taken away all my clothes?

Adam They want to make double sure you stay.

Michael Oh my God, I am chained to a wall.

Edward So you are. So are fucking we. So you better enjoy it.

Michael What do you mean, 'enjoy it'?

Edward It's a laugh, isn't it, Adam? That's how we get by. Laughing at it all. Do you not enjoy a laugh? Have you no sense of humour?

Adam Stop freezing the guy out.

Michael How long have you been here?

Adam Four months.

Edward Two months.

Michael My name is Michael. Michael Watters.

Edward So what's up in the outside world, Mick? Do you mind me calling you Mick? Is there much word about us?

Michael I'm sorry?

Edward Do people talk about us? Have you heard anything about our people? What are they doing to release us?

Michael I don't know.

Edward What do you mean, you don't know?

Michael I had barely arrived in Beirut, I really wasn't well acquainted with anyone –

Edward People must have been talking about us –

Michael People would mention in passing –

Edward 'Mention in passing'? Do they know what we're going through?

Adam Are we forgotten?

Michael They get on with their lives. If they thought too much about it, about you, they'd – they'd –

Adam What?

Silence.

They'd what?

Michael I don't know. I really don't know anything about the political situation in Lebanon. I came here to teach English. I lecture in English. That's all. That's why I was asking people round to dinner. To learn the ropes a little. I was going to the market. I wanted to buy pears for dessert. They stopped me. They had guns. I was so frightened. I told them I was simply a teacher of English at the university. I was so frightened. God, where am I? Please, let me go. Let me go.

Adam That's enough. You mustn't let them hear you cry. They're listening to you as you speak. They want you to weep. Don't ever do that in here. I'm warning you, don't weep. That's what they want. So don't cry. Laugh. Do you hear me? Laugh.

Michael I can't.

Adam Laugh, damn you.

Michael No.

Edward starts to laugh loudly. He stops. Adam laughs loudly, Edward joining in. They stop.

Adam Go, Michael. Laugh.

Silence.

Laugh.

Michael laughs.

More.

Michael laughs more loudly. Adam and Edward join in his laughter. They stop. Adam signals Michael to continue laughing. He does so.

Good guy. That's what you got to do. They've heard you laughing.

Michael What will they do now?

Adam Wait and see.

Silence.

They're in a peaceful mood tonight.

Edward They're not even laughing back.

Adam Mission accomplished, Michael. Stage one.

Michael Who are they?

Edward The enemy.

Adam The food's OK. We are given a bottle of water each day. They let us use the bathroom, but they go with us. We are never alone. We've managed so far. We are always in these chains, that is so degrading. We are given the Bible and the Koran to read. But the worst of all is that we have no way of knowing what is going on in the outside world.

Edward We can't even listen to the BBC World Service.

Adam No, we can't.

Edward No contact with the outside world; that goes about its business.

Adam That's the way it is in Chinatown.

Silence.

Edward Are you a married man?

Michael Widowed, I'm afraid, some years ago. No children.

Edward Any dogs?

Michael *A* cocker spaniel and a golden retriever. They're at my mother's home. Near Peterborough. She lives –

   Silence.

She lives there. Near Peterborough.

   Silence.

Adam I was a doctor.

Edward You still are. Journalist, me.

Michael I lost my university post. They're not teaching much Old and Middle English these days. A dying concern. Rationalisation of resources. They say. So when I could only get employment here, I came here. I absolutely need to work. I was warned about the danger. I was worried. But I refused to be afraid. So I came here.

Adam And got caught.

Michael Yes.

Edward Yes.

   Silence.

Are you all right?

Adam You'll get used to it. In time.

   Silence.

Edward Who was coming to dinner?

Michael I'm making a pear flan.

   Silence.

I thought everything was going very well, very well indeed, but just when I'm about to pop it into the oven, gas mark seven, I discover I can't find the pears. The pears. I'd forgotten the pears.

Lights fade.

SCENE THREE

Edward browses through the Koran. Michael sits with his eyes closed. Adam is running on the spot.

Adam I wish we could go to see a movie.

Edward Uum.

Adam Jeez, I'd enjoy a good movie.

Michael Yes.

Edward Do you like pictures?

Michael I do.

Edward You might have struck me more as a book man.

Silence.

Michael I do enjoy a good book as well.

Silence.

I would prefer at the moment to see a movie.

Edward Why are you calling them movies? Do the English not call them films?

Michael I just called it a movie. Why do you object?

Edward It just sounded strange.

Michael Oh, sorry.

Edward Why are you sorry?

Michael That I didn't call it a film, if it offended you.

Edward It didn't.

Michael Then why did you bring it up?

Edward Something to say.

Adam stops running.

Adam I wish we could go to see a movie.

Edward You've said that. We've heard you.

Adam Yeah.

Silence.

Michael I don't think I'd like to be a film star.

Edward Why not?

Michael I imagine being an actor is quite a boring life.

Edward Yeah.

Adam Yeah.

Silence.

Edward Aye, boring.

Adam Yeah.

Michael Yes.

Edward No.

Michael No.

Edward What do you mean, 'No'? You've just said yes.

Michael I was agreeing with you. I thought you were agreeing with me. So I said no.

Edward You say no when you're agreeing with someone?

Michael If they've said no, yes.

Edward Yes or no, what is it?

Michael What?

Edward Shut up.

Silence.

Let's see a movie. Shoot the movie. An Englishman comes to Lebanon.

Adam Being well trained in the social graces, he invites people to dinner. He does not necessarily like these people, but they speak English, and they would seem to know the ropes about this place, so they may help him to endure his time here. He will feed them. There is only one problem. Food. He will take his courage in both hands and walk through the city of Beirut looking for food to cook. To his surprise he sees at some distance from him the very same people he has invited to dinner. He calls to them, but they don't answer. He calls again, he follows them, and they are going into districts of Beirut he does not know. He follows them, he finds himself trapped, he sees them ahead of him, still he calls out. They look back. They leave him. The film ends.

Silence.

Hitchcock. That's who made that movie.

Edward I can't stick Hitchcock.

Adam Why?

Edward His endings.

Adam Yeah.

Silence.

Shoot another movie.

Edward A nun comes to Beirut. She has come to do her Christian duty to the orphans of that troubled city. She first befriends a goat wandering through this war-torn town. She greets the goat as a long-lost ally, singing to it on her guitar. Little children hear her song and join in, miraculously learning English. Our happy band join forces, they fight the cruel foe, they convert the whole of Lebanon to the great task in hand – love thy neighbour. Not everyone is pleased with Sister's success. She is shot, as is her guitar. One of the little children presses the bullet-strewn instrument to her body as they carry away the corpse of the dead nun.

Adam Played by Madonna.

Edward As they carry off the corpse, vultures gather. They eye the dead nun hungrily.

Adam They swoop in their throng down on the dead body. They start to tear her flesh. A band of machismo Arabs arrive on white steeds. The horses' flesh contrasts in their beauty with the shattered flesh of the dead virgin. They draw their guns. The shoot off the vultures' heads.

Edward Sam Peckinpah Productions.

Michael In the midst of this horror music is heard. A man preaching peace moves through this machismo crowd. He is dressed in a loincloth. He speaks against violence. He speaks of civilisation. He is a man of peace.

Adam Richard Fucking Attenborough movie.

Edward Fortunately at that moment a crowd of peasants dance on to the scene, waving scythes. Immaculately photographed, they win the hearts of the cruel Arabs, for among the peasants there is one disabled who has a dream – to be an artist. With the help of his mother, and his own determination, he finally wins an Oscar, which he collects with his ear –

Adam Oh Jesus, not an Irish movie, please –

Edward And they live happily ever after.

Silence.

We're fucked.

Michael So it seems.

Edward How are you feeling?

Silence.

Come on, give us a dose of the stiff upper lip. Raise our morale, old boy. Tell us all about the war. So many chappies went through what we're going through. Fine example to us all. Let's hear it for the British!

Silence.

You're a miserable git, aren't you? There's not much life in you. Is there?

Silence.

Michael I'm no more afraid of you than I am of them.

Edward Stiff upper lip, let's hear it for –

Michael I mean it. I'm not afraid of you.

Adam He's not afraid of you, Edward.

Edward He's not afraid of you, Adam.

Adam He's not afraid of anything.

Edward No, he's not.

Michael In this dreadful situation –

Edward In this dreadful situation –

Michael Where we have found ourselves –

Edward Where we have found ourselves –

Michael I fail to see how tormenting me –

Edward I fail to see –

Michael Will in any way alleviate –

Edward Alleviate – alleviate – alleviate – alleviate – alleviate.

Michael Do you wish me to admit I'm afraid of you?

Silence.

Is that what you wish me to do?

Silence.

Would that in some perverse way help you to be less afraid yourselves, because you are both very afraid, and I find it distinctly repulsive that you turn together against me for the sole reason of backing each other up in your fight against them. We are in this together. Don't forget that. If I go under, so do you.

Silence.

Adam Shoot the movie.

Edward There were three bollockses in a cell in Lebanon. An Englishman, an Irishman, and an American. Why they were in that cell was anybody's guess, and why they were in Lebanon was their own guess.

Adam The American was the first to be caught. While he was on his own, he was frightened of going mad.

Edward The Irishman was second to be caught. He would have went mad without the American. They were joined, these two bollockses, by a third bollocks, an Englishman.

Michael The Englishman did not know if being in the cell in Lebanon had driven the other two mad. What has happened to him in being kidnapped strikes him as being madness, so he has attempted not to lose his head in the face of severe provocation –

Edward In not being afraid of them he's convinced them they have not gone mad.

Adam And in their way, in so far as is possible, they thank him for that conviction.

Silence.

Michael You both scare the shit out of me.

Edward English people always scare the shit out of me as well. As for fucking Americans –

Michael Yes, they are all quite mad –

Edward Can you imagine what it was like to land in here with that Yankee –

Michael Yes, it must have been worrying –

Adam What the fuck is this?

Michael I do wish we could stop swearing. My language has gone to pot since meeting you both. I really do feel that we are giving in to them if we allow ourselves to descend to vulgarity – no, I'm being a sanctimonious prig. I apologise.

Silence.

I'd also just like to say that I think Richard Attenborough's films are quite good. He spent over twenty years trying to make *Gandhi,* and it's a testimony to his decent, well-crafted and honourable political views –

Edward Michael?

Michael What?

Adam Shite.

Michael Well, it was a bit long, the film of *Gandhi.*

Silence.

Adam I wonder what Sam Peckinpah would have done with the life of Gandhi.

Edward Gandhi would have been shot in the first reel.

Michael Actually, Gandhi is shot in the first reel of Richard Attenborough's film.

Edward Is that a fact?

Michael Yes.

Silence.

Are there any vultures in Lebanon?

Adam What do you mean?

Michael Well, in the film where Madonna is eaten by vultures, would that be realistic in Lebanon?

Silence.

That was meant to be a joke.

Silence.

Vultures are much maligned creatures, you know. I'm not an expert myself on their dietary habits, but I did once hear on *Round Britain Quiz* a fascinating description –

Adam Michael, I am Sam Peckinpah. This is a gun.

He points his finger at Michael.

You are dead.

He shoots Michael.

Edward What a senseless waste of human life.

Michael Do you think we'll ever get out of here?

Silence.

What can they possibly gain by holding us hostage?

Silence.

My mother isn't terribly well. She'll be very worried about me. Do you think they will have at least let her know I'm alive? I know it may not sound very sensible to be worried about one's mother when we're in the position that we're in, but I do worry, I worry so much – I was just wondering if they would have told her not to worry –

Adam I'm sure they have.

Edward Yes.

Michael Yes.

Silence.

It is quite worrying, isn't it?

Edward Yes.

Michael Yes.

Adam It's just as well you're not afraid.

Silence.

Michael We could be here a long time, couldn't we?

Silence.

Adam That was my major reservation about *Gandhi*. It was too long, that film. Very long.

Lights fade.

SCENE FOUR

Adam rocks himself to and fro, gently, humming 'Someone to Watch Over Me'. Michael sits wide awake, alternating his gaze from Adam to Edward. Edward sleeps.
Edward mumbles in his sleep. Adam whispers to himself.

Adam Mama and Papa, Mama and Papa, Mama, Papa.

Michael It's extraordinary how little sleep I need in here. You haven't been sleeping terribly well either, Adam.

Adam Adam's won a scholarship, Adam's Phi Beta Kappa, are you proud of me?

Adam continues singing 'Someone To Watch Over Me'.

Michael Edward, of course, is dead to the world.

Adam No, they were too busy, too many foster kids, got to look after the foster kids. We welcome in our house all our unfortunate little brothers and sisters. Do your bit to build a new America. So they thought, while the rest of America was flushing itself down the toilet. And Adam is such a help to us.

Michael How were you a help?

Adam Adam is bright. Maybe he's too bright. How could he be too bright? Adam worries too much. If we let him, he'd take on all our worries. Get rid of your worries, folks, get rid of the foster kids. Get rid of the fucking foster kids. Oh God, help me. I want to – what do I want? Sleep – just sleep. I can't. Because when I sleep, I dream. I dream of my mother and my father, and I hear all the fights in that fighting house. I dream of my girlfriend. I dream of her family. I dream of myself. And I am so scared, because I no longer recognise myself in this dream. God help me. God help me. Get me out of here. Please, please. There, there, baby. Be quiet. I'm here, I'm here, your mama's here. She's strong. Your papa loves you. Please keep your sanity, kind, good Adam, we need your strength so much.

Silence.

Michael I am sorry to see you in pain. Shall I waken Edward?

Adam No.

Michael I wish he were awake.

Adam How long have you been here?

Michael Four weeks and three days, I'm keeping a count.

Adam Do that, yeah. The first month you keep counting. And the second month. In my third month, Edward came. And so you get to know him, fourth month. He gets to know you the next month. Then you want to kill him. Or you want to kill yourself. And the worst month, this month, you don't want them to kill you. What you want is to go home. All the time, want to go home. Want to hear one American, any American voice, apart from your own. How dare you? I'm an American. How dare you do this? I'm an American.

Edward wakes up.

Edward Adam, what the hell is this?

Adam How dare you hurt me like this?

Edward What's wrong with him?

Michael He's an American.

Edward Come on, Adam, come on.

Adam What have I done to you?

Edward It's me, it's Ed, it's me. Michael's here. It's us.

Silence.

You're all right. You're all right.

Silence.

Adam I've got to keep myself looking good.

Michael You look terribly well, Adam.

Silence.

Adam They won't harm us. We're their most valuable asset.

Michael I find some consolation in that, you know. When I lost my university post, I did feel redundant. You see, I devoted a large part of my life to building up a department, and hey presto, one wave from the wicked witch's wand, and it's gone. So it's nice to feel valuable. Wanted in some way.

Silence.

Pathetic, isn't it?

Adam What is an American?

Edward Someone born in America.

Adam An American is, I repeat, a valuable asset. A prize possession. Prized, yes, valued, but not loved. There is a price permanently placed on the American's head. And in his head the American believes the value of the price placed upon him, because his is a market economy, and in that economy everything has a price. But that same market decrees the price may differ in day-to-day dealing. And the valuable asset, the prize possession, this American, has no control over his price. Whoever has no control is fucked. I am American, I am Arab, I am fucked. We have that much in common.

Silence.

How did your wife die?

Michael Nita? An accident. Life was different without her.

Silence.

But Nita certainly would not have wanted me to turn into a weeping willow, so, one got on with sweet life as if, well, nothing happened. Something had happened. Professionally, I changed. Before her death I was full of ideas for publications. Nothing terribly exciting. Mostly on English dialects. Anyway, after the incident, I simply read the Old English elegies and the medieval romances, and I taught as best I could. I published nothing. I'd lost my wife and my ambition. My lack of publications didn't help at the time of the rationalisation. Well, these things happen.

Edward That's cheered us all up.

Michael It wasn't intended to cheer you up. It wasn't even intended for your ears. I was speaking to Adam, who asked me a question. Are you feeling a little better, Adam?

Adam No, I hate these shorts.

Michael There isn't much we can do about that.

Adam I want a pair of jockey shorts. I want to wear my country's greatest contribution to mankind. Fresh, white jockey shorts. A man's underwear. That's why Arabs can't wear them. If their shorts don't have a hole in them, they can't find their dicks. I want a pair of jockey shorts. I want to kill an Arab. Just one. Throw his body down before his mother and father, his wife and kids, and say, I did it, me, the American. Now you can blame me. You are justified in what you do to me. You have deserved this. I want to see their faces fill with hate. True hate. I want that within my power.

Silence.

Fetch me the Koran that I may read of power.

He reads from the Koran.

In the name of God, the Merciful, the Compassionate.
Behold, we sent it down on the Night of Power:
And what shall teach thee what is the Night of Power?
The Night of Power is better than a thousand months;
In it the angels and the Spirit descend,
By the leave of the Lord, upon every command.
Peace it is, till the rising of dawn.

Silence.

Peace it is, the Night of Power.

Silence.

Peace in the house, when the foster kids are sleeping. Everyone at peace, except Adam in his head. His head is hot. He forgets his manners. He shoots off his mouth. He hurts. Forgive me, my sisters and my brothers, for doubting if you were sisters and brothers. Forgive me, my foes, for calling you my foes. In your good book lies the way to power and to peace.

He kisses the Koran.

I am come into my garden, oh beloved.
Thou that dwellest in the gardens, the companions
    hearken to thy voice: cause me to hear it.
Make haste, my beloved, and be thou like to a roe or
    to a young hart upon the mountains of spices . . .
Ah but my beloved, why do you turn aside from me?
I am my beloved's, and my beloved is mine.

Edward Well, will we write our letters?

Adam Is it time?

Michael What letters?

Adam Home.

Michael Will they post them? Will they give us pen and paper?

Edward Teach him, Adam.

Adam No, you go first. You write to your wife.

Edward Dearest wife, what is your name again? That was a joke. There is no address at the top of this as I don't know where I am, but then I never did, as you would say. You know I'm not a great one for writing letters, but I know you'd want to hear from me, I hope. I am doing well and bearing up and trust you and our family are doing likewise. There are now two other men with me, Adam the American, who is getting married soon and we will be at his wedding if we have to sell the house; and Michael, who is an Englishman. Enough said. I can no more understand why I am here than you can. It is a terrible thing to keep a man or woman from their family when they have done nothing. All right, maybe I was a fool to come to this country, but I wanted to, and you would never stop me – that is why I – that is you all over. Tell the boys to keep supporting Manchester United. Forget Liverpool. Up United. Tell them also their sister is the best footballer of the three of them. And why? Because she is a dirty wee bollocks. Beautiful, but bad. Like her father. I thought I would leave you laughing, and I only wish I could hear you, your husband, Edward.

P. S. What do you mean, Edward who?

Adam That's pretty good, Edward. Michael, you want a go?

Michael Dear Mum, I am very well. I am sorry that circumstances have prevented me phoning you every Sunday, as promised. I share accommodation with an American and an Irishman and so I am often flooded by a torrent of emotions, which I rise above. The guards who are attending us are terribly distant. The nearest I've met to them are our awful neighbours, the snooty Shawcrosses. Fortunately the Shawcrosses don't carry guns and knives. I hope the new vicar is working out for the best and has abandoned the idea of folk singing and clog dancing at the harvest festival. Please don't be tempted to try either. Edward, the Irishman, is interested in soccer. I hope Peterborough United are doing well, for, as you know, I follow soccer as well. I am writing this letter on the first of the month. You always said rabbits on the first of the month. For luck. So, rabbits. For luck. Your loving son, Michael.

Oh go ahead, Edward. Start straightaway.

Edward Start what?

Michael Attack me for writing to my mother. Pansy little Englishman. I don't mind. I've had it before. I can tell you, there were people who were surprised I got married. Look at him sitting there smirking.

Edward I did not open my mouth.

Michael I read it in your letter. Dear wife, dear children. Support Manchester United. It's enough to make me vomit.

Edward Did I open my mouth against him?

Michael Sitting there, gloating –

Edward Would you like me to stand up and dance a jig?

Michael I buried my wife. I can't write to her. I heard that letter. It was an attack on me.

Edward You were far from my mind.

Michael 'There's an Englishman with us. Enough said.'

Edward You came into this cell –

Michael It is not a cell. I am in a room. I have never been inside a prison and I never will be. How dare you put me in a cell?

Edward You came into this room then –

Michael This room, yes.

Edward We tried to help you.

Michael Help me? How? You throw your wife into my face. You throw your children in my face. I have neither. Yes, you've succeeded. I've failed. That's what you're really saying, isn't it?

Edward Adam, you started this caper, stop it.

Michael He will not stop it. You mock me for writing to my mother.

Edward Listen, boy, we're sitting together on death row, and what concerns you, stupid bastard? That I'm mocking you, when I have not, you English –

Adam Arab? English Arab? Irish Arab? Right, guys? Jesus, these guys don't need to tear us apart. We can tear each other apart.

Silence.

Can I write my letter now? Is it my turn?

Silence.

Dear folks, here I am, still in the shit. We have been joined by an English guy, called Michael. Edward is fine. I am bearing up. No, I am not. Forgive me if this upsets you, babes, but you know how I mentioned that I sometimes feel like a hunted animal, even though I am caught in this cage. The hunters seem to be getting closer. I can smell their guns. One night I dreamt that I had died. You were looking down at me. Papa, you reached out to touch my dead body, and when you touched me, I came back to life. I hope this dream comes true. I am going to die. There are nights when I listen to the silence and I think we are all of us going to die. I don't know what I am going to do. The only time we may leave the cell is to go to the toilet. They normally do not let us close the bathroom door. This time the Arab guy slammed the door shut. I stood there for a long time. When they threw open the door, there were three of them, waiting for me. And one raised his hand and pointed his finger at me.

Adam does so.

I have been selected to go first. Since this happened, my head has not really been right. Maybe I just imagined this. But I feel that finger pointed at me, and I am very scared. I love you both, Adam.

Silence.

Guys, what am I going to do? They got my ass over a barrel, and I ain't wearing jockey shorts. I smell oil.

They're going to cream my ass with oil, and they're going to fuck me dead. Up my ass, baby. Up my ass. Will they kill me for oil?

Silence.

So, it's the first of the month, Michael?

Edward I won't let them. They won't kill you.

Adam Say rabbits. For luck. Say it.

Michael Rabbits.

Adam Rabbits. For luck. Rabbits. Rabbits.

Lights fade.

SCENE FIVE

Edward sits wide awake. Adam sits, crouched, humming 'Someone to Watch Over Me', reading the Koran. Michael lies sleeping.

Edward Wake and sleep, wake and sleep, what else is there to do, eh, Michael? What are you dreaming of? Mammy in Peterborough? Are you dreaming of us, Michael? Are you?

Silence.

Do you feel like a bit of exercise, Adam?

Adam continues humming.

Are you still asleep, Michael?

Adam In the Name of God, the Merciful, the Compassionate.

Edward Look at him. Sleeping like a big baby. Happy in his nappy. I think he's less cross than when he came in here. Maybe he's stopped teething.

125

Adam

In the Name of God, the Merciful, the Compassionate.
We have sent the Koran on thee.
Remember the name of the Lord.
You cry lies like the voice of Doom.
But over you there are watchers,
Over you there are watchers,
Watchers, over you, over you.
We have sent the Koran down on thee,
Remember the name of the Lord.
Say to unbelievers, I serve not what you serve,
And you are not serving what I serve,
But to you, your religion, and to me, my religion.
To you, your religion, to me, my religion.
In the Name of God, the Merciful, the Compassionate.

silence.

Edward To you, your religion, and to me, my religion?
The Koran?

Silence.

Save us from all who believe they're right. Right, in the
name of God who is not merciful and not compassionate,
for he is like them, always right. I've seen it at home
before. Scared wee shits, panting with fear, ready to make
the big sacrifice. They must be right, for if they're wrong,
God help them. And if they're right, God help us. It's the
workings of the world I fear, and my fate it is to fear,
said the blind man screwing his mother.

Adam I hope she enjoyed it.

Edward In the Name of God the Merciful, the
Compassionate.

Adam And if he's not?

Edward Then he's not.

Adam What are we going to do then?

Silence.

What are we going to do?

Edward Be men.

Adam And do what?

Edward Face up to your fate.

Adam And then what?

Edward Defy it. Defy them. Fight them. Never show pain in front of them.

Adam Never.

Edward Never.

Silence.

Adam I think what first started to drive me mad in this place is not knowing what time of day it is. I think it's night.

Edward I know it is.

Adam Are you afraid of the dark?

Edward There's been darkness in this room. I've felt the enemy surround me in the dark. Listening, waiting for me to crack, to cry. They think I'm in their power. I am, the three of us are. They decide if we live or die. It's up to them. But there is still one thing left up to me. Me alone. Have they, or have they not, made me less of a man, by reason of what they've done to me? And they haven't. They've made themselves less than men, in locking me away like this. No matter what cause they are doing it for they have still made themselves less than men. But I want to say this, I am a better man than any of them, for I would not torture them like this. That is

127

my choice. They do as they're ordered. I do as I choose. Locked in chains, for all to see, but not beaten down to the ground yet. In the Name of God, the Merciful, the Compassionate.

Silence.

Adam We're at their mercy.

Edward We're at our own.

Adam Our fate?

Edward Face it, I said. Face it.

Silence.

Adam Will you be able to look after Michael? He's growing more and more frightened.

Edward He's learning to fight his corner.

Adam He won't be able to.

Edward Do you think he was married at all? What did a wife see in him?

Adam What did your wife see in you?

Edward More than a drink of water, I can tell you.

Adam He'll need you.

Edward Let's stop this chat. Why are you already acting as if you're not here? Wise up, boy. You're still a valuable commodity. We are their prize heifers. You keep the same heifers for display. And rest assured of one thing. If the boys out there bump you off, I won't be long after you at the pearly gates. If I'm left alone with Michael, I'm bumping myself off.

Adam Commit suicide? You? Never.

Edward Don't bank on it. You've never been to an NUJ union meeting. The slowest form of suicide known to man.

Michael Are you talking about suicide?

Edward Were you not sleeping, you bollocks?

Michael I've just woken up. Were you saying something about suicide?

Adam Have you tried it?

Michael I certainly thought about it after Nita's death. She reasoned me out of it.

Edward You saw her ghost?

Michael Don't be so ridiculous. There is no such thing as ghosts. I simply had an imaginary conversation with her. As usual, she gave me excellent advice. I did as advised.

Adam Which was?

Michael Make my pear flan. She adored my pear flan.

Edward If I hear one more word about this fucking pear flan –

Michael Honestly, the Irish have the most attractive accent but their coarseness is so self-defeating. Without it, I do believe they would have the most beautiful dialect of English.

Edward Dialect?

Michael Hiberno-English can be quite a lovely dialect. Those Elizabethan turns of phrase, those syntactical oddities, which I believe owe something to Gaelic, the sibilants –

Edward You called it a dialect.

Michael It is a dialect. Hiberno-English.

Edward What I speak is not a dialect of English.

Michael Then what do you call it? Portuguese?

Edward Call my language what you like. It is not a dialect.

Michael You are a profoundly ignorant man.

Edward Am I? Listen, times have changed, you English mouth, and I mean mouth. One time when you and your breed opened that same mouth, you ruled the roost, you ruled the world, because it was your language. Not any more. We've taken it from you. We've made it our own. And now, we've bettered you at it. You thought you had our tongues cut out, sitting crying in a corner, lamenting. Listen. The lament's over. We took you and your language on, and we won. Not bad for a race that endured eight hundred years of oppression, pal, and I speak as a man who is one generation removed from the dispossessed.

Adam Edward, you had a university education. You live in a more than comfortable home. You earn a large salary. How in hell are you dispossessed?

Edward One generation removed, I said. And there are those I hold responsible for that dispossession. Him, being one.

Edward points at Michael.

Michael There is not much historical validity to that charge.

Edward Remember the Famine? The Great Hunger?

Michael The Irish Famine was a dreadful event. I don't dispute its seriousness. But I'm sorry. How can I be personally responsible for what happened then? It was a hundred and fifty fucking years ago.

Edward It was yesterday.

Michael You are ridiculous, Edward.

Edward I am Irish.

Michael Then may I ask you Irish one question, if I am personally responsible? I am a little troubled by the Famine. Could it be you only had your silly selves to blame?

Edward Adam, I'm going to knife him.

Michael You left yourselves utterly dependent on the potato. Why didn't you try for a more balanced diet? Carrots are delicious. What about bread and cheese?

Edward Jesus.

Michael That's typical. That is so Irish. Call on Jesus to solve your problems. Well, what if you had called on Jesus, and he said, 'Turn Protestant'? What would have happened then?

Edward Some of us did turn Protestant.

Michael And what happened to them?

Edward We ate them without salt.

Michael Quite nutritious I hope they were too.

Adam Guys, give me a break.

Michael I was provoked. You heard him.

   Silence.

What you accused me of was unfair, but I did say things that were unthinking, as did you, and you did accuse me personally.

Edward I accused you of nothing.

Michael Adam is my witness. You held me personally responsible for eight hundred years of persecution.

Edward That was a joke. Have you no sense of humour?

Michael I have an excellent sense of humour.

Edward You have as much sense of humour as my arse.

Michael Then my sympathies to your arse being stuck with you.

Adam Guys, please, guys.

Michael It's preposterous. He does nothing to alleviate this dreadful situation. There are times I believe he is on their side out there. I have done nothing to offend him. Yet he attacks me, knowing how distressed I am when I don't know if my mother is alive or dead, and I don't know if I'm going to live or die. We could at least maintain the semblance of civility in this dreadful . . . dreadful . . . Quite preposterous. If your intentions were to annoy me, you have succeeded admirably.

Silence.

I apologise for that dreadful outburst. I may have put us all at risk by that dreadful outburst.

Silence.

I have said some very stupid things.

Silence.

Edward I was stupid.

Michael Selfish. As I was. We're not thinking of Adam.

Edward Adam's fine.

Michael Of course Adam is, but if Adam, wishes to complain –

132

Edward Adam will.

Michael Adam is too –

Adam Hey, fuckers, Adam's here. He can speak for himself.

Michael Of course you can, Adam.

Edward Right you be, Adam.

Adam So shut it. For as long as you are here, I am here. OK?

Silence.

Michael It would be wonderful to be released together, wouldn't it? You must promise to come to Peterborough and see the cathedral. I do believe it is the most glorious building in all of England. When I was a boy I really did think God lived in it.

Edward Good enough football team, Peterborough United.

Michael Edward, they've never been out of the fourth division.

Edward One year they made the third. Kicked out, weren't they, some scandal over money?

Michael We don't talk about it.

Edward I'm still surprised you're a supporter.

Michael One has a certain loyalty.

Edward Yes, I know. Dear old dirty Dublin. When you come there, I'll take you round it on the Dart. It's a train that runs along the coast of Dublin, from Howth to Bray. Howth to Bray. Raheny, Harmonstown, Connolly, Tara, Sandymount, Booterstown, Booterstown – Jesus, to see those names, to say them. There's a bird sanctuary

at Booterstown. Kingfishers fly there. I saw one once.
I pointed it out to my daughter.

Silence.

Can you remember birds singing?

Silence.

The Birdman of Alcatraz, that was a great film, wasn't
it?

Adam Alcatraz is near my home. When I take you to
San Francisco, to Fremont, we'll cross the bay and go to
Chinatown, where they have the best fish restaurants in
America. Lobster, lobster, and more lobster.

Silence.

It's going to be OK.

Silence.

It's all going to be OK.

Michael Do you know that no one has ever precisely
explained the etymology of OK?

Edward My, have they not?

Michael My favourite theory is the Stonewall Jackson
one. You may have heard this, Adam. It concerns the
American Civil War –

Edward A lot of Irishmen died in that war.

Michael Mostly fighting to retain slavery.

Edward Give me proof of that.

Michael *Gone with the Wind.*

Edward What?

Michael With a name like Scarlett O'Hara she was hardly from Knightsbridge.

Adam Just give us the Stonewall Jackson theory, Michael.

Michael It's said he never learned to read or write, so when he got papers to sign, he always put OK at the bottom, because he spelt 'all' with an 'o' and 'correct' with a 'k'.

Edward Couldn't read or write, could he?

Michael So they say.

Edward Completely illiterate then, was he?

Michael That would follow, yes.

Edward If somebody is completely illiterate not merely can they not spell, they also cannot mis-spell. If he couldn't read or write how would he know about an 'o' or 'k'?

Michael Yes. That shatters the Stonewall Jackson theory somewhat.

Edward It does, somewhat.

Michael Theory is so dangerous in all academic matters. Now take linguistics itself –

Edward What have I started?

Michael I lost interest years ago in modern linguistics. All that heated debate over the Bloomfield–Chomsky controversy. It's all so dated now. Chomsky's theories themselves –

Edward Have disappeared up their own arse.

Michael Yes, they have, actually.

Silence.

Edward I'd love a cigarette. I'd love a drink.

Michael I could murder a cup of tea.

Silence.

Edward Fuck it, I'm breaking out, I'm having a drink. Anybody joining me? Adam, first shout, what do you want to drink?

Adam A beer.

Edward How about a little Martini?

Adam A vodka Martini then.

Edward Twist or olive, sir?

Adam Twist *and* olive. I'm a mean vodka Martini man.

Edward Michael, what are you having?

Michael Just a sherry, please.

Edward A sherry? All right. Sweet sherry?

Michael Medium, please.

Edward One small medium sherry coming up.

Michael Oh, what the heck – make it a large one.

Edward Yes, what the heck.

Adam Hey, do I detect the fragrance of an exotic substance passing from hand to hand through this distinguished company? Pass it here. And I'll have another vodka Martini.

Edward Coming up, sir. And I'll have the same. Cheers. (*Roars.*) Hold it. Quiet.

Michael What is it?

Edward Listen. Do you hear. Close your eyes. You'll hear it. The door, it's opening. Somebody's coming in.

Silence.

It's them. They've heard us enjoying ourselves. They know we're drinking. Keep your eyes closed. They're here. They're watching us. They're angry. Do you see them?

Silence.

They don't approve of this. They're going to stop us. What are we going to do?

Silence.

Adam Drink.

Silence.

Edward Drink?

Michael Drink.

Edward Drink.

They down the imaginary drinks.

We haven't done as we're told. We've got them in a state of shock. They're ours for the taking. What will we do with them? Look, boys, at this. A full keg of Guinness. Enough to drown a man. Will I drown them with drink? Will I drown them? Will I?

Silence.

Michael It would be rather a waste of the Guinness.

Edward Good man, Michael, you said it. So will we let them sit down? Will we make space for them? Do you invite them to the party?

Adam nods.

Take the weight off your feet, boys. Imagine it's a wedding, or as near as makes no difference. Bit of a song. A story.

The same the world over. Have a drink if you like. We won't tell. Join us.

Adam Will they?

Edward Up to them. In the Name of God, the Merciful, the Compassionate. To you, your religion, and to me, what? What to me? To the happy day I'm let go, alive. Cheers, men. Just for the night, celebrate. Come on. Will you join us?

Michael What are they going to do?

Edward Staying. They love a song, Arabs. They've heard we're great singers.

Edward sings 'The Water Is Wide':

The water is wide, and I can't cross o'er,
And neither have I wings to fly.
Give me a boat that can carry two,
And both shall row, my love and I.

For love is gentle and love is kind,
And love is sweet when first it's new,
But love grows old and waxes cold
And fades away like morning dew.

There is a ship and it sails the sea,
She's loaded deep, as deep can be,
But not as deep as the love I'm in,
I know not how I sink or swim.

Adam joins Edward in the song.

Adam *and* **Edward**
The water is wide, and I can't cross o'er,
And neither have I wings to fly.
Give me a boat that can carry two,
And both shall row, my love and I.

At the song's conclusion, Michael rattles the chains, Edward and Adam following suit. Suddenly there is silence.

Edward It's quiet back there. The Arab boys must have slipped out.

Michael Did they enjoy themselves?

Edward They didn't say.

Michael Their rudeness takes my breath away.

Edward These boys never say anything. Their strength depends on silence. Careless talk costs lives. That's scrawled on every wall from Belfast to Derry. The nearest I ever really came to anything like the same boys, I was driving to Newry, there had been some other outrage and, foolish man, I stopped to give this, what I thought was a down-and-out, a lift. He got into the car, and then I saw he was carrying a rucksack. I said nothing about the rucksack, I tried to make general conversation, but no go. Not a word out of him but yes or no. I finally asked him, What's in the rucksack? He looked at me and he said, Mind your own fucking business. The sweat started to break out on me. We were coming near to a police checkpoint, so I stopped the car and asked him again about the rucksack. Mind your own fucking business, that was his reply. I said, Get you and your rucksack out of my car. He opened the door, run like hell, and left the rucksack lying there. The sweat was now blinding me. I opened – I opened the rucksack. I opened it.

Michael What was in the rucksack?

Edward Mind your own fucking business.

They laugh lowly, Michael still looking confused.

Michael Edward, what was in the rucksack?

Edward Michael, it's a joke.

Michael Oh I get it, I get it. There was nothing at all in the rucksack. Very good. (*Laughs.*) Very amusing, Edward.

Edward Time for the story. Mick, you're in the good form. Tell it.

Michael There's a terribly sad story in Old English. It's a poem, called 'The Wanderer'.

Edward We want a happy story.

Michael There's a very happy story in Middle English called 'Sir Orfeo'. It's really based on Ovid's Orpheus myth, and the variations from the classical sources reveal the essential optimism of the medieval mind and its profound faith in human happiness to triumph over despair. I find that mind so much deeper than Renaissance doubt. It can be so destructive at times, doubt. It has its place, lack of faith, and I myself suffer from it at times –

Edward Are you going to tell us the story?

Michael Long ago there lived a knight called Sir Orfeo who married a lady called Herodis, and they loved each other. They lived in England, in Winchester, actually. Medieval poets tend to set the ancient myths in familiar places. Part of their charm. Where was I? Yes, Herodis was full of love and goodness, no man could describe her fairness. One day Herodis slept under the shade of a magical tree and, to cut a long story short, she was stolen by death who came to her as a king, the King of the Underworld.

Edward Did he live in Winchester as well?

Michael The Isle of Wight, actually. Don't be facetious. She was stolen by death. Orfeo, who, by the way, was a great musician, wept for his wife and went into the forest, there to lead a living death, for he knew whither thou goest, I will go with thee, and whither I go, thou shalt go with me . . . Yes, yes . . . He entered hell and played music, and won back his wife, and returned safely to Winchester. Thus came Sir Orfeo out of his care. God grant us all as well to fare. Amen.

Edward Very nice, Michael.

Adam Really great.

Michael Is there any more drink?

Edward Sherry?

Michael I think I'll try a vodka Martini.

Edward Three vodka Martinis coming up. Catch, lads. Cheers.

Adam Cheers.

Michael Indeed. Quite delicious.

   Silence.

Edward So, Adam, you're being quiet. A quiet man.

Adam (*sings*)
   Amazing grace, how sweet it sounds,
   That saved a wretch like me.
   I once was lost but now am found,
   Was blind, but now I see.

   Through many dangers, tall and stern
   We have already come.
   We have this day to sing God's praise,
   Than when we first begun.

Amazing grace, how sweet it sounds,
That saved a wretch like me.
I once was lost, but now I'm found,
Was blind, but now I see.

Silence.

Michael Thank you.

Edward Thank you.

Adam Thank you.

Lights fade.

SCENE SIX

Michael is eating his meal from a bowl. Edward lets his food sit untouched beside him. The chain that held Adam lies empty.

Michael This is good. (*He eats more in silence.*) It's chicken. The vegetables are fresh as well. A bit overcooked for me. Undercooked for you, I'd say. But it's good.

Silence.

Aren't you going to eat? You must be hungry.

Silence.

You haven't eaten for three days. They're getting worried about you not eating.

Silence.

This not talking, this not eating, isn't going to help us. We are in a decidedly perilous position, to put it mildly. You might say, Put nothing mildly. But we can't push them too far. Push them as far as we can push them, is that it? Then they are liable to turn very nasty indeed.

They are in quite a state as it stands. They know what they have done. At the moment they are hovering between apology and arrogance. Trying very hard as I am to take some rational – some comfort out of this, I do feel they themselves did not wish to kill Adam – He is dead. I have evidence of that, as have you. My evidence is that one of them actually wept –

Silence.

That's an act he was putting on to mock us, is that what you think? One of them wept when he came into this – this cell. There is no point in believing that. That's a lie? A complete lie? Don't fall for that, yes? They have him in hiding somewhere else? Your main worry is that he may be on his own. He did manage on his own when they first got him. He will manage now. But you are not eating until he is brought back here to us? He is not dead? You firmly believe that. Nothing I can say will convince you otherwise? Do I understand you?

Silence.

Edward They would not kill him.

Michael What would he have done to stop them?

Silence.

Adam is dead, Edward.

Edward You want him dead. You feel safer with him dead. One of us down, and no more to go. With him dead there'll be a big outcry and we will be saved. Isn't that it? Well, listen, get that out of your head, for if they've put him down, they can put us down as well. Dogs together, to be shot. Take no consolation from imagining him dead. It won't save you. It won't save me.

Michael No, it won't save you. You hope it might save you, but you're perfectly correct, his death won't save you.

143

You condemn yourself out of your own mouth. It isn't me who wants him dead. It's you, isn't it?

Silence.

I don't blame you for thinking that. You want to give his death some – some sense of sacrifice. You are in grief, in mourning. And you are mad with grief.

Edward He is not –

Michael (*roars*) Dead, he is, and you know it.

Edward You know nothing.

Michael I know about grief. About mourning. How it can destroy you. I know.

Silence.

You know he's dead, don't you?

Silence.

Say it, he is dead.

Silence.

Edward He died. I needed him. Jesus, I needed him.

Silence.

How could he leave me? How could he do this? Without him, how will I get through this?

Michael Bury him.

Silence.

Remember him.

Silence.

What was he like?

Edward He was gentle. He was kind. He could be cruel,
when he was afraid, and while he was often afraid, as
we all are afraid, he was not often cruel. He was brave,
he could protect himself, and me, and you. He was
beautiful to look at. I watched him as he slept one night
I couldn't sleep. He moved that night through his sleep
like a man not dreaming of what life had in store for
him. He was innocent. Kind, gentle. Friend. I believe it
goes without saying, love, so I never said. He is dead.
Bury him. Perpetual light shine upon him. May his soul
rest in peace. Amen.

Silence.

Michael
    Love bade me welcome: yet my soul drew back,
      Guiltie of dust and sinne.
    But quick-ey'd Love, observing me grow slack,
      From my first entrance in,
    Drew nearer to me, sweetly questioning,
      If I lack'd anything.

    A guest, I answer'd, worthy to be here:
      Love said, You shall be he.
    I the unkinde, ungratefull? Ah my deare,
      I cannot look on thee.
    Love took my hand, and smiling did reply,
      Who made the eyes but I?

    Truth Lord, but I have marr'd them: Let my shame
      Go where it doth deserve.
    And know you not, sayes Love, who bore the blame?
      My deare, then I will serve.
    You must sit down, sayes Love, and taste my meat:
      So I did sit and eat.

Silence.

Edward I'm hungry.

Michael Then eat.

Edward Dear friend.

Edward eats.

He's dead.

Michael We are not.

Lights fade.

SCENE SEVEN

Michael is looking from side to side. Edward watches him. Michael claps his hands. Edward remains silent. Michael gasps. He resumes looking from side to side. He applauds again.

Michael Great shot.

Edward More fool me for asking, but what the hell are you doing?

Michael Ssh, I'm in the middle of a very important rally.

Jumps to his feet applauding.

Oh well played, Virginia, well played.
　　Now they're changing ends I can answer your question. I am reliving the 1977 Wimbledon Ladies' Final. Virginia Wade of Great Britain against Betty Stove of Holland. The Queen in her Silver Jubilee Year is attending Wimbledon for the first time. The poor dear is bored to distraction, but Virginia is going for a British win and the excitement is mounting. Excuse me, the third set is about to continue. I'm going to serve.

Michael starts to play a tennis match.

A perfect ace. Virginia is really getting on top of things now. What do you think, Dan Maskell? I'm not counting any chickens before they're hatched, but I think we should be practising a few bars of 'For She's a Jolly Good Fellow'. Oh I say, a wonderful shot. Come on, Virginia. Oh dear. He who hesitates, or in this case, she who hesitates, can lose all. Oh I say, another winner from Virginia.

Edward For the love of Jesus.

Michael What do you mean, 'For the love of Jesus'?

Edward What are you up to?

Michael Do I complain when you relive great horse races the Irish won? Great football games? Great rugby? I enter the spirit of things. Cheer along. So should you.

Edward I'm just feeling sorry for poor wee Betty Stove.

Michael Poor wee Betty Stove is six foot and weighs twelve stones.

Edward Her mother still thought of her as poor wee Betty.

Michael Her mother is irrelevant. Virginia is playing to win and is going to win.

Edward That's unfair.

Michael That's history.

Edward To hell with history, I'm rooting for Betty. Who's serving?

Michael I am.

Edward Take it away, Virginia.

Michael goes to serve, tossing back his head four times.

What are you doing?

Michael It's a tense moment in the match. Virginia always tossed her head at a tense moment.

Edward It's distracting.

Michael It's a habit.

Edward It's a bad habit. You shouldn't . . .

Michael suddenly serves.

Michael Another ace. My game.

Edward What do you mean? I wasn't ready.

Michael My game.

Edward I wasn't ready. I appeal to the umpire. What should I do, Adam?

He looks to the empty chain. Silence. Edward suddenly adopts a loud American voice.

You cannot be serious. You cannot be serious. Are you blind? Are you stupid? This is the pits. God damn it.

Michael I think you'll find John McEnroe was not involved in the 1977 Ladies' Final.

Edward What do you mean? I'm Betty Stove and I was just asking a question. Can you give me an answer? I'm only asking . . .

Michael A little-known fact about Virginia Wade is that in her youth she was a boxing champion. She applies a neat one-two to Miss Stove and sends her spinning. This is the first Wimbledon Final ever to be settled on a knock-out. Virginia has done it. Virginia has won Wimbledon. Virginia will have tea with the Queen. Your majesty.

Michael curtsies.

Edward What?

Michael Your Majesty. Present me with the award and say something.

Edward I'm now the Queen?

Michael Yes.

Edward Hello.

Michael Hello.

Edward Here you are.

Michael Thank you.

Edward And what do you do?

Michael What do you mean, what do I do? You've just seen me win Wimbledon.

Edward Oh yes, it was very nice.

Michael Thank you.

Edward You must sweat a lot playing tennis.

Michael I must, yes.

Edward Is this your racket? It's quite sweaty, I like a little sweat.

Michael The Queen is not into sweat.

Edward Why not? The smell of sweat is a well-known turn-on.

Michael That's enough! Can I have my racket back?

Edward With pleasure.

Michael Ah, I'm exhausted after those three tough sets.

Edward Yes, you must be.

Silence.

Michael You're quite a hairy man, Edward. I've just noticed that. Have you ever tried the chiffon scarf test?

Edward Immac?

Michael Ah, you're old enough to remember Immac Hair Remover? A friend of mine was quite disturbed by his body hair. So when he read about Immac he bought some in his local chemist. He told the lady behind the counter it was for his mother. It worked, the Immac. But when he tried the chiffon scarf test – you know, shave one leg with a razor, use Immac on the other leg, the chiffon scarf ought to fall off the Immac leg, but it didn't on this occasion. He hadn't let the Immac set. It stuck to his legs, the scarf. The screams were dreadful. This is true. It did happen to a friend of mine.

Edward What age were you when this happened?

Michael Seventeen, I'm ashamed to say. How did you know it was me?

Silence. Michael sings:

Run, Rabbit, run, Rabbit,
Run, run, run,
Here comes the farmer with his big gun,
He'll get by without his rabbit pie,
So run, Rabbit, run, Rabbit,
Run, run, run.

Silence.

It's actually quite fun if one of us pretends to be the rabbit.

Silence.

Shall I be the rabbit and you sing?

Silence.

Edward
Run, Rabbit, run, Rabbit,
Run, run, run –

Michael scurries about on his chain.

What the hell are you doing?

Michael I'm impersonating a rabbit.

Edward You don't look remotely like a rabbit.

Michael You could do better?

Edward Sing the song.

Michael sings as Edward impersonates a rabbit:

Michael
Run, Rabbit, run, Rabbit,
Run, run, run,
Here comes the farmer with his big gun,
He'll get by without his rabbit pie,
So run, Rabbit, run, Rabbit,
Run, run, run.

Edward Now that's what I call a rabbit.

Michael You looked more to me like a kangaroo.

Edward How the hell did it look like a kangaroo?

Michael impersonates Edward impersonating a rabbit.

Michael
Run Rabbit, run, Rabbit,
Run, run, run –

Edward I did not look remotely like that.

Michael You did, you know it was ridiculous.

Edward I did not start this ridiculous business in the first place.

Michael No, no, you didn't.

Silence.

Edward When I was covering the troubles at home I interviewed this Derry woman. She'd had her windows broken, I asked her in my innocence – I was a cub reporter – to sum up the situation. She said, 'Son, this whole situation can be summed up in two words. Ridiculous. Ridiculous.'

Michael Is it really our fault for your troubles at home? Is it the English people's fault?

Edward Ridiculous.

Michael Is it our fault we're here in the first place?

Edward Ridiculous.

Michael Do those children holding us captive have a reason to hate us?

Edward Ridiculous.

Michael Sum up our situation in two words.

Edward Christ, help us.

Michael That's three words.

Edward Jesus, look down on us.

Michael Five words.

Edward God and His Blessed Mother, help us.

Michael Ridiculous.

Edward Yes.

Michael Ridiculous.

Silence.

Edward They think we have no faith, the Arabs. They are ridiculous.

Michael And have we faith?

Edward Do you want proof?

Michael Yes. Give it to me.

Edward Who won the 1977 Wimbledon Women's Final?

Michael An Englishwoman won it.

Edward I rest my case that there is a God.

Michael Well done, Virginia.

Edward Well done, Virginia.

Michael Poor wee Betty Stove.

Edward There always has to be a loser. In every game, a loser.

Michael Yes, that's history.

Edward (*sings*)
    For she's a jolly good fellow,
    For she's a jolly good fellow,
    For she's a jolly good fellow,
    Which nobody can deny.

Lights fade.

SCENE EIGHT

Edward is exercising strenuously. Michael exercises less strenuously.
    Edward belts out a song.

Edward
    Jingle bells, jingle bells,
    Jingle all the way.

Michael breathlessly sings.

153

Michael
Oh what fun it is to ride
On a one-horse open sleigh.

Edward
Hurrah for dear old Santa Claus,
Hurrah for Christmas Day.

Silence.

Michael I'm finding it a little easier now to do ten push-ups.

Edward Good for you.

Michael I do find I'm growing a little fitter. Isn't it dreadful the way a sedentary job ruins the body?

Edward exercises frantically. He suddenly stops.

Edward You're sure it's Christmas Day?

Michael Nearly certain.

Edward Is it day or night?

Michael I can't tell.

Edward We should be safe on Christmas Day, even if they don't celebrate it.

Michael Yes, of course.

Edward I'm getting out of here. I'm leaving.

Michael You can't. You're chained to the wall, Edward.

Silence.

I can guess what's coming now. You're going to get thoroughly silly and totally upset. Please, do not mention your family. It won't make things any easier for either of us if you do insist on remembering them.

Silence. Edward sings.

Edward

>Oh come, all ye faithful,
>Joyful and triumphant,
>Oh come ye, oh come ye, to Bethlehem.

>*Silence.*

And in the manger is the Christ child. Who has caused all this bother for us. Do you realise that? If we'd been born Muslims, this wouldn't have happened. So it's his fault. Or our fathers' fault and our mothers' fault for believing in him.

>*Edward sings.*

>Oh come, all ye faithful,
>Joyful and triumphant,
>Oh come ye, oh come ye, to Bethlehem.

>*Silence.*

Passing the time on a Christmas Day. Peace on earth, goodwill to all men. Peace, what's peace, Michael?

>*Silence.*

Peace is lying beside a woman. Touching her, by accident, all soft. Smelling her, not stinking like us. Listening to her breathing. That's the only sound she makes, in the peace. Her breath. Listen, listen. Peace together, as she sleeps, and me awake, lovely, lovely. I would press against her belly, and kiss, and I would be happy as a lark. Her legs move as she sleeps and I hold them, and want to lift them and conceive in the morning, on Christmas Day in the morning, in the happy, happy bed, our bed. Wife. Wife. But who's here but you, Michael?

>*Edward laughs.*

There are times the sight and sound of you disgust me. I can feel a smell off you. Sickening. The sight of you sickens me. The sound of you. I find your smell sickening.

Michael Did you sleep with Adam?

Silence.

Did you?

Edward No.

Michael Did you want to?

Silence.

Edward No.

Silence.

Do you believe me?

Michael You didn't have the chance. If you'd had the chance, if you hadn't been chained, if I hadn't been here, would you have slept with him?

Silence.

If you had known he was going to die, would you have slept with him?

Silence.

Beautiful to look at. Kind, gentle.

Edward No. I would not have slept with him.

Silence.

I would like another child. I want another child.

Michael Yes.

Edward I need to be a father to my children.

Michael Yes.

Edward What if I don't come out alive? Anything can happen. I smoked over forty cigarettes a day before these shites got me. I could have cancer. Don't laugh at me. It's

156

curable, even lung cancer, if they get it in time. My da died from it, and there's no doctors here. You see, Adam was my great security. If there had been anything wrong with me, he had the doctor's gift of the gab. I trusted him. He would tell them I was a sick man. I need to go home. I was planning that at Christmas. I want to go home, Michael. It's Christmas Day. I want to be at home.

Michael My father was absent at Christmas. For many years. He was a prisoner, during the war. He returned as a stranger.

Silence.

He remained a stranger, poor man. He would never talk about the war. It was not his way to talk. He died, he died because of the suffering he'd endured during the war. I could never tell him to me he was a hero. That suffering, his suffering, was not for nothing. But my father – to know my father – to love my father –

Michael avoids Edward's gaze.

Would you excuse me?

Edward I will, yes.

Silence.

Michael Sometimes they talked quietly about the war, or my mother did rather. How very frightened people were, but couldn't show it. Bred into us, that, I suppose. Don't show fear, even if you're a coward. I never cried as a child, I still don't cry . . . Yes, yes. One night, out of the blue, I'd fallen asleep, and I woke up on my father's lap. He was weeping in front of my mother, and he was saying to her, You must not tell him what it was like there, you must never tell him. And I felt the most terrible pain in my ear. I thought my head was going to explode with pain. I kept on listening, although even then I knew he was telling her something about the war, the camp I presume, and I should not have heard anything. He kept saying her name, her name, repeating it, all the time. I said, I am awake and I have a pain in my ear. He rubbed my ear. He said, There is a place called Sparta. Brave soldiers come from there. When they have pain, they show it by controlling it. Don't be afraid of pain. Don't be afraid of controlling it. You have been raised by a strong woman. The bravest men sometimes behave like women. Before the Spartans went into battle, they combed each other's hair. The enemy laughed at them for being effeminate. But the Spartans won the battle. That was really the only conversation we ever had. I was old enough to remember every word.

Silence.

I did have one other conversation with him. It was after his death. I was reading an Old English poem called 'The Wanderer'. A man sits alone in a desolate, frozen landscape, remembering when he had friends, when he had dreams, and now he is deserted. And I heard my father. I heard his faith. And I heard him in that ancient poem, speaking with the voice of England, talking to itself, for the first time. Our beginning, our end, England's. One line haunts me. *Oft him anhaga are gebideth.* I've tried for so long to understand it fully. I think it means, 'A man who is alone may at times feel mercy, mercy towards himself.'

Silence.

We long for our dear life, lamenting great loss – my father is dead – but accepting fate. *Wyrd bith ful araed.* In the same poem. *Wyrd bith ful araed.* Fate is fate. When I read 'The Wanderer', I feel possessed by my father. I feel for him, and for England. I love my country because I love its literature very much. I am proud to have taught it. That pride and, yes, I mean pride, is the reason I can sustain my sanity here. Most loved mother, remember me . . . most loved missed father, pray for me . . . most loved missed wife, most loved wife . . . Rather me were to lose my life, than thus to lose . . . wife. Ridiculous. Her death was ridiculous.

Michael laughs.

Edward What happened to her?

Michael Ridiculous.

Edward How did she die?

Michael A car crash. She was driving to work. It was the month of May. I wasn't with her. I was revising an article at home. I answered the phone and the university told me she was unconscious, at the scene of the accident. I knew. I sat by the phone. Half an hour later they rang to say she was dead. I went to identify her. She looked like a child who'd fallen off her bike. It was me persuaded her to buy a car. We were both working. We could afford a car. Full of love and goodness. Gone. Such is life. I slept for some time afterwards with the bedroom light on. Then one night I switched off the light. Gone. Happy Christmas, Edward.

Edward Happy Christmas, Michael.

Michael I never learned to drive.

Edward I'm not fucking surprised, sunshine.

Michael Cheery little soul, am I not?

Edward What do you want for Christmas?

Michael I'm being given a present?

Edward Anything you want, sir.

Michael Well, I actually could do with a face flannel.

Edward I don't believe this.

Michael It's most inconvenient without one.

Edward We've had the shits in this hole, we've no contact with any belonging to us, we have nothing – I'm offering you the world on a plate, and what do you ask for? A face flannel.

Michael I'm a man of simple tastes. I don't ask for much.

Edward Well, for being a good boy, I'm going to give you something special. Look, it's a car.

Michael This is in dreadfully bad taste, Edward.

Edward A new car. Hop into it.

Michael I've hopped.

Edward Switch on the ignition.

Michael Roger. What now?

Edward The best way to teach someone to drive is to let them find their way into it at their own pace. What do you think you do next?

Michael I put my foot down on the little thingy.

Edward Put your foot down on the little thingy.

Michael And I steer with the steerymajig?

Edward The steerymajig.

Michael And if I want to go faster I press this little fellow?

Edward You do.

Michael And I release it to drive slower?

Edward You do.

Michael My God, it's moving, it's moving. I'm driving a car. I'm actually driving a car. Look at me, driving a car.

Edward Wave to the people, they're cheering you.

Michael waves regally.

Michael I'm as drunk as the Queen Mother.

Edward I don't want to alarm the Queen Mother, but look behind you. You'll see we're being followed.

Michael Who by?

Edward The enemy. Drive like hell, they're firing guns.

Michael Do I press the little fellow?

Edward Press, press, press. They're gaining on us.

Michael I'm pressing, I'm pressing.

Edward Go for it, man. Faster, faster. Think of Steve McQueen in *The Great Escape*.

Michael What did he do?

Edward He got caught. Fuck him. Forget Steve McQueen. Just go faster.

Michael Oh my God, Edward, I can't control the steerymajig. It's taking over me. It's got a life of its own. We've got to go where it takes us. Will I keep my foot on the thingy?

Edward Keep your foot on the thingy.

Michael Edward, the car's started to fly. It's flying. We're in a flying car.

Edward How can a car fly?

Michael
Oh you, Chitty-Chitty Bang-Bang,
Chitty-Chitty Bang-Bang we love you,
And our Chitty-Chitty Bang-Bang,
Chitty-Chitty Bang-Bang loves us too.

Edward joins in.

Both
Heigh-ho, everywhere we go,
On Chitty-Chitty wheels we say,
Bang-Bang Chitty-Chitty Bang-Bang,
Our fine four-fendered friend,
Bang-Bang Chitty-Chitty Bang-Bang,
Our fine four-fendered friend.

Michael Whee!

Edward Where are we?

Michael Flying over the sea. We're leaving this place behind us. Look, Edward, it's Europe. I can see France, and Germany, and Italy. Oh, doesn't Europe look so lovely? Hello, Europe, how are you? Did you miss us? Look, Edward. Down below. It's England. You can see the coast of England. I believe it's Dover. And there are bluebirds over the white cliffs of Dover.

Edward I know. One's just crapped on your head.

Michael I don't mind. And up north we travel from Dover. Passing London. Why, there's the Houses of Parliament and all who dwell in them, who've left me to rot in a cell in Lebanon. Shall I crap on them, or shall I not waste a good crap? I shall drive on. I can see the spire I'm looking for. Down we go, Chitty. Come on, Edward. We're going to Peterborough. Do you see the cathedral? I'm going to do something I've always wanted to do. I'm going to let Chitty drive to the very top of the cathedral and look down on it from inside the roof.

Edward No, you're not.

Michael Yes, I am. It's very daring climbing to the rooftop. The public normally aren't even allowed on the third level.

Edward Get me down, I've no head for heights.

Michael Look at the wonderful west front. The hand of God. Glorious architecture. I do apologise for the stained glass. Victorian. Awful. Well, pretty in their own way, but I'm being generous.

Edward Get me down.

Michael Don't panic. You're in safe hands. I had a terrible fear of driving, but you taught me to conquer it, and with you in the car beside me, I feel quite safe.

Edward I've news for you. I can't drive either.

Michael screams.

Michael We're falling. We're falling.

Edward Keep turning the steerymajig, keep your foot on the thingy.

Michael I've got my foot on it.

Edward Don't touch the little fellow.

Michael I'm not laying a finger on him.

Edward I can't look. What's happening?

Michael It's all right, we're flying again.

Edward Good man, Chitty-Chitty, good man.

Michael I think Chitty-Chitty might be a girl.

Edward Where's she heading for now?

Michael She's flying west, over England, she's passing Birmingham, and Liverpool, you take over. Tell me where we are.

Edward Jesus, I can see it, home, Ireland. Look at it. The shape of it. The colour. Green, it is green. I can see the colour green again. Good girl, Chitty-Chitty. Keep going. Down, down, down. Have we landed?

Michael Yes, safely.

Edward Then drive.

Michael Where?

Edward Just drive. It's Christmas Day. Drive me to where we go on Christmas Day. I want to wander through the rows of graves. I want to see his, my father's grave. I have to talk to him. That's all. Talk to him.

Silence.

Da, it's me. It's Edward. Your son, do you remember? Do you recognise me?

Silence.

I've been away for a while, Da. Do you know me?

Silence.

Son, I'm going to die, son.

Silence.

Da, you'll never die. Never.

Silence.

Yes, I will die, son.

Silence.

You'll outlive us all, Da.

Silence.

Will I go to hell, son?

Silence.

There's no such place as hell, Da.

Silence.

Pray for me. Pray for me.

Silence.

I won't see through this night. Do you hear the way I'm breathing?

Silence.

Yes.

Silence.

Yes, I hear the way you're breathing.

Edward sings.

Tell me a story,
Tell me a story,
Tell me a story and then I'll go to bed.

Silence. Edward laughs.

Do you want anything, Da? Anything at all? Tell me a story, tell me . . .

Silence.

The priest comes to see me, son. He's saying Masses. Pray for me. Will I go to hell?

Silence.

There is a hell, Da. And I'm in it. I am very scared, Daddy. Please save me. Please get me out of this place.

Carry me in your arms away from here. If you're in heaven, will you save me?

Michael Laugh, Edward.

Edward They've beaten me.

Michael They really have beaten you.

Edward Save me.

Michael They can hear you crying. Laugh.

Silence.

Laugh, you bastard, laugh.

Silence.

Laugh.

Lights fade.

SCENE NINE

Edward is free from the chain, dressing himself. Michael watches. There is silence.

Edward Being an Irishman helped me. I don't know what kind of deal the government would have done.

Michael Yes.

Silence.

Edward I'll go to see your mother first thing.

Michael Do that.

Edward I'll tell her you're well.

Michael Yes, please. Put her mind at rest.

Edward I will.

Silence.

Michael Edward, if she's dead –

Edward She's alive, Michael.

Michael She is. Please give my best wishes to your wife and family and tell them how I look forward to seeing them.

Edward I will. I'll tell them all about you.

Michael Do.

Edward I'll remember everything.

Michael I'll miss you.

Edward And I you.

Silence.

Will you be all right?

Michael Me, despair? Never. Remember, I support Peterborough United.

Edward True enough. They're letting me go because of Adam. They need a bit of good publicity, I'd say. He's going to save us, he's watching over us –

Michael You're free, and I'm here.

Silence. Edward puts on his tie.

Edward I never wear these things normally. Better put on a good show. They beat me down, didn't they?

Michael Yes, they did beat you down.

Edward I don't know what I'll do when I get out.

Michael Go easy on yourself. Don't drink too much.

Edward I won't. I promise. We should be let go together.

Michael We're not.

Edward Yes.

Michael When you cried, you were heard. I wasn't.
Maybe I didn't cry hard enough. Maybe they think
I haven't suffered enough. Is that what all this is for?
To see us suffer? And to what end? What is it for? I don't
know. I never will. Do you know in all the time I've been
in here I have never once dreamt that I was locked in?
Always in my dreams I'm free. A free man. And I would
really like my dreams to come true. Will you tell them
that? Maybe the dreams will change without you here.
Maybe I won't be able to sleep even.

Edward You will. You have to. You have to keep up
your strength. You're the strongest man I know. I'm –
I'm not. I need you. For what it's worth, I'm watching
over you.

Michael That much I know.

Edward Sleep, dream.

Michael I will. Move, or they might change their minds.

Edward Right, right.

*From his jacket pocket Edward takes out a comb.
Edward goes to Michael. Edward combs Michael's
hair, and gives the comb to Michael. Edward bows his
head. Michael combs Edward's hair. Michael gives
Edward the comb.*

Right.

Michael Right.

Edward Good luck.

Michael Good luck.

Edward leaves. Michael stands still. His body convulses. He regains control. Silence.

Oft him anhaga are gebideth. Wyrd bith ful araed.

Silence.

Whither thou goest, I will go with thee, and whither I go, thou shalt go with me.

Silence.

Right. Right. Good luck

He rattles the chains that bind him.

Good luck.

DOLLY WEST'S KITCHEN

For Phenie Franklin Mac Gabhann

Dolly West's Kitchen was premièred by the Abbey Theatre, Dublin, on 1 October 1999, with the following cast:

Dolly West Donna Dent
Rima West Pauline Flanagan
Esther Horgan Catherine Byrne
Justin West Michael Colgan
Ned Horgan Simon O'Gorman
Anna Owens Lucianne McEvoy
Alec Redding Anthony Calf
Marco Delavicario Perry Ojeda
Jamie O'Brien Harry Carnahan

Director Patrick Mason
Designer Joe Vanek
Lighting Nick Chelton
Fight Director Richard Ryan

The play was subsequently produced at the Old Vic Theatre, London, in May 2000

Characters

Dolly West, in her thirties
Rima West, her mother, in her sixties
Esther Horgan, her older sister, in her late thirties
Justin West, her brother, in his twenties
Ned Horgan, Esther's husband, in his forties
Anna Owens, the Wests' maid, in her late teens
Alec Redding, in his late thirties
Marco Delavicario, in his twenties
Jamie O'Brien, Marco's cousin, in his twenties

Place

Buncrana, County Donegal,
near the border with Derry

Time

During World War II

Setting

The Wests live in a large, comfortable three-storey
house that overlooks the beach and is near the pier.

It is immaculately clean, well presented and colourful.

To one side of the house there is a very large garden
that is being thoroughly utilised and well tended.

The herb garden is the only part of this visible on stage,
but it stretches to include substantial vegetable patches,
fruit-bearing trees and bushes and chicken coops.

At the centre of the stage is the kitchen itself.

The kitchen is dominated by a large, well-scrubbed
wooden table.

The living room, called the good room, is upstairs,
out of sight.

The family live in the kitchen. If at all possible,
the table should represent the heart of the kitchen.

There will be an obvious need for chairs, cutlery, glasses,
mugs, etc., but nothing should detract from the table.

To the other side of the kitchen are the shore and the sea.

The house is always present to the sound of the sea,
and between Act Two, Scene One and Scene Two
the whole stage is transformed into a shore/seascape.

It might be possible, if useful, to begin the play
with that shore/seascape lifting to reveal
the kitchen and its immediate environs.

Act One

SCENE ONE

There is a large white bowl on the table. Dolly West cracks an egg into the bowl. Anna stirs the egg. There are scones of bread on the table.

Dolly Beat the egg gently.

Anna Am I doing it too fast?

Dolly Yes. Take your time.

Anna It makes a lovely colour, the yolk and the white. Is this egg Hetty's?

Dolly How would I know?

Anna Your mother knows them all by name. Great name, Hetty the hen, isn't it? She's my favourite. She knows her own mind. If she wants to lay an egg, she will. Have I beaten it enough?

Dolly Stir it once more – for luck.

Anna How is that lucky?

Dolly An old Italian custom – they do it for wedding cakes. Do the same with all the other eggs, one by one.

Anna Did you love Italy, Miss West?

Dolly I wasn't in it long enough. Six or seven years in Florence, and I'm home four years now. I'm beginning to forget it. I loved Florence all right. Running a restaurant there was rough work. You begin to forget the reason for going to live there in the first place.

Anna Why did you go there?

Dolly I studied the history of European painting in university. I wanted to learn more. No better place than Italy.

> *During all of this Anna is breaking and stirring the eggs.*
> *Dolly has started to sort out herbs and different leaves of lettuce.*
> *She expertly eyes them, but disregards little, leaving them to soak in a white basin of water. What she keeps she washes thoroughly, laying them to dry on a yellow dishcloth.*

Anna I'd love to go to Italy and get married by the Pope. Beautiful. The only thing would ruin it is wearing black on your wedding day.

Dolly Black?

Anna A black mantilla. All women have to wear it meeting the Pope. Imagine destroying a white wedding dress with that contraption on your head instead of a veil.

Dolly Will you wear a veil, Anna?

Anna With the rationing these days? Miss West, I know a girl saving to get married next Boxing Day, she asked her mother about getting a veil. Her ma said she would be lucky to pull the skin of her arse over her head.

Dolly Will you marry, Anna?

Anna With all those American soldiers stationed across the border in Derry? They're the last word. They come over to the Republic when they're on leave and they're not supposed to, but the women all latch on to them. Even if they weren't gallivanting about and I didn't get married, it wouldn't be for want of asking.

Dolly I'm sure it wouldn't. You're a lovely girl, Anna.

Anna beams with pleasure.

Anna I'm not – I'm wild-looking.

Dolly You're a beautiful girl, Anna. (*She carefully seasons the eggs.*)

Anna Why did you never marry, Miss West?

Dolly I was never one for walking down the aisle.

Anna But you've stepped out with fellas – in your day? Between the two of us?

Dolly I might have – in my day – and I might have done more than stepping out. Between the two of us.

Anna Miss West, if a fella you take a shine to you and asks you for a feel, should you let him?

Dolly Feel what?

Anna You know yourself.

Dolly No, I don't know.

Anna You must know.

Dolly I don't.

Anna Jesus, you must at your age.

Dolly Is it your nose? Feel your nose, pick your nose?

Anna What?

Esther enters by the shore.

Dolly Anna, if any man wants to pick your nose, don't let him. It's a disgusting habit.

Anna I wouldn't let anybody pick my nose.

Dolly Then you're a wise woman.

Esther comes into the kitchen.

Anna I think you've spent too long in Italy, Miss West. Men don't do that here.

Dolly A credit to Irish manhood.

Esther What's to Irishmen's credit?

Dolly They don't pick women's noses.

Esther They would if there was a bottle of Guinness up them.

Anna I happen to think Irishmen are a credit to their country.

Esther You should marry one. I happen to think they're full of it.

Anna Full of what?

Esther Raspberry jam. Imagine your wedding night, Anna. You're lying there looking at the ceiling and he comes at you with his cockadoodledandy. (*She makes the sound of an explosion.*) He covers you in raspberry jam. It's the happiest day of your life.

Dolly I'll tell that Ned Horgan on you.

Esther You tell my husband what you like.

Anna I think Mr Horgan is a good man.

Esther An excellent man. An excellent soldier. Defending Ireland from invasion, a neutral man in a neutral army protecting his neutral wife.

Dolly Anna, my mother's in the garden – see if she wants tea.

Anna exits.

Watch that mouth of yours – Anna's no more than a child.

Esther I can't help what I say. My mind's on this war.
We're living in a port, Dolly. Buncrana is a port. Our
beloved leader, De Valera, has warned this part of the
country they might invade us for our ports, coming at us
from all sides, the English, the Germans and the Yanks.
The English we've dealt with before – we can deal with
them again. What about the Germans?

Dolly Start praying it's the English.

Esther And the Yanks?

Dolly They're full of raspberry jam – full of it – we
could eat them all.

Esther Now I could eat a horse. What are you cooking?

Dolly Eggs just – and a salad.

Esther Lovely. Justin and Ned are eating with us.

Dolly I thought they'd be eating in Dunree fort. I've no
meat for them. They'll be like bears.

Esther Let them eat what's put in front of them. There's
plenty of scone bread to feed them.

Dolly The men will want potatoes at least.

Esther Jesus, you'd think they were royalty.

Dolly Anna, dig us some spuds from the garden.

Anna calls offstage.

Anna All right.

Dolly Did you find Mammy?

Rima enters the herb garden.

Rima What did you mean, did you find Mammy? Was
I lost or what? Where was she to look for me – under a
gooseberry bush?

Esther Need a right size of gooseberry bush to find you under it.

Rima Maybe it was the one you crawled out from.

Esther Did you really find me there, Mammy?

Rima You're a bit long in the tooth to believe that, aren't you? You know well how I got you. A coal boat came to the pier and it delivered you. I washed you. I dried you, I clothed you in silk, Esther, my eldest born. Look at you now – I should have dumped you back in the water. Dolly, are we eating eggs again? I want none of that green stuff floating about in that bowl.

Dolly Mother, that's herbs.

Rima Mother, that's shite. The amount of grass and leaves we eat in this house – it's not natural. That whore Hitler's doing me out of a bit of stewing beef. The men won't eat that. I won't either.

Dolly You have to eat – if it's not eggs, what do you want?

Rima A slice of the cat's arse, please.

Dolly You've cut that many slices off the cat, it has no arse left.

Rima Maybe in fancy Italy you ate cats. This is Ireland. We've known true hunger. A hundred years ago we *were* eating the very grass. Now Dolly West is doing it to us again. Look at the face on her. She's so miserable you'd swear she was a Derry woman.

Dolly Thank you very much.

Rima Say what you like about this war, the siege of Derry was worse. They were eating the rats. Lundy sold the city for the sake of a bun. That's how starving they were, the Derry people. Of course, at that time they were all Protestant. I've always heard it prophesied we'll see them begging again with their mouths open for bread.

Dolly Who prophesied that?

Rima Our Lady when she appeared in Moville. Years before yous were born. They got very big-headed about that. Then Our Lord Jesus Christ appeared around the shore front in Buncrana. That put a stop to Molville's gallop.

Esther What did he prophesy?

Rima How would I know? He didn't appear to me. The one who did see him, she wasn't much use – she was deaf and dumb.

Esther Could she talk and hear afterwards?

Rima They say she could but who knows? She was put into a convent, or maybe it was a mental home? I don't know. I will have a mouthful of those eggs, even if they kill me.

Dolly I might find you a rat to go with them.

Rima The eggs will be enough to poison me.

Dolly Mother dear, I would not poison you. That would be too slow.

Rima What did you say?

Esther She said you were getting a bit slow – a bit old.

Rima She'll still feel the whack of my fist if she doesn't watch herself.

Justin and Ned enter from the garden, Ned in sergeant's uniform, Justin in officer's.

Ned Who are you threatening, Rima?

Rima You and all the Irish army put together, Sergeant Horgan. Good afternoon, Justin, darling son, head buckcat of the Irish army.

Rima sings the opening lines of the Irish National Anthem.
Justin grunts, opens his newspaper, sits and reads it. Ned cuts a slice of scone bread, butters it and eats.

Good afternoon, how are you, Mother? I'm well, son, is there anything in the paper? A plague of killer bees are heading towards Buncrana. Son, what will the Irish army do? Give us all your sheets, Ma, we'll spread syrup over them and hang them on the washing lines! That way you'll be saved. And so will we, the men of Ireland, because of my mammy's syrup. My son, Justin, my son the officer – he has brains to burn. Honest to Jesus, other women give birth to children. I gave birth to three mad whores, one uglier than the other.

Justin I am not ugly.

Esther We are not ugly.

Rima Thank Christ I'll never have to marry any of yous. Dolly, ask your brother, the colonel-in-chief, why he has a face like a hatchet?

Anna enters with a basin of washed potatoes. Dolly starts to examine them.

Dolly What's wrong with you, Justin?

Justin Nothing wrong as yet. Have you not got the spuds on? We haven't got all day for our dinner.

Dolly Less than twenty minutes they'll boil. Why are you like a bear with a sore head?

Ned We had a phone call at the fort this morning. It was from your old pal Alec Redding, Dolly.

Dolly Alec – where is he?

Ned Across the border – stationed in Derry. He's in the British army.

Dolly I guessed that much. Why's he in Derry?

Ned Working with the Americans – some kind of interpreter.

Dolly The Americans speak English.

Justin That's a matter of opinion.

Rima I cannot follow what the Yanks are saying in films. I spent the whole of *Gone with the Wind* getting Esther to tell me what are they saying – what are they saying?

Esther Will I ever forget it?

Rima What was wrong with Vivien Leigh anyway, wanting that drink of water, Leslie Howard – what was wrong with her? She had Clark Gable . . .

Justin We were talking about Alec Redding.

Rima When is he coming down to see us?

Ned Well, he would definitely like to –

Dolly Of course, he will. Alec was always welcome –

Justin Was.

Dolly What do you mean 'was'?

Justin No man will be welcome here wearing the uniform of the British army. If you all want to meet, take the train to Derry. Meet him across the border in the so-called Northern Ireland.

Dolly So you're now decreeing who sits in this kitchen?

Justin No British soldier will come under this roof. It's bad enough we have to tolerate them in the North. They've laid claim to that, but not for much longer after the war's over.

Dolly Justin, this is Alec.

Justin I don't care if it's God almighty.

Anna I wouldn't worry about him being in uniform, Mr West. If the soldiers cross the border, they have to wear civvies. The British soldiers are very good about it. The Yanks, though, you always see them in uniform. I don't blame them. Their trousers are gorgeous.

Justin When I ask for your opinion, you can open your mouth. Gorgeous trousers.

Dolly Did Alec say when he'd come down?

Ned The weekend – Saturday or Sunday.

Justin Are you going to defy me?

Dolly Defy you? Who do you think you are, pup?

Justin The man of this house who chooses not to let an enemy soldier into his house.

Esther His house –

Justin An Irishman who does not want the English anywhere.

Dolly I didn't know you'd signed your house away, Mother.

Rima I haven't.

Dolly Then what do you say?

Rima I couldn't give a tinker's curse who comes in here, just as long as they don't attack me in my bed. Mind you, Alec's not a bad-looking man. He can attack me wherever he likes.

Justin You're setting some example, Ma. Many Irishwomen were attacked in their beds by British soldiers.

Rima And many were throwing their leg over more than a bicycle.

Justin You should be ashamed –

Rima Son dear, would you get off your knees praying and dance? It would be the life of you. Why are you not out chasing women?

Silence.

Justin Dolly, if you welcome Alec into this house –

Dolly If you don't welcome him, you don't eat. Starting now, you starve, boy.

Justin Throw your dinner into the fire. The fire –

Ned Justin, be a good man, sit down and eat –

Justin Are you telling me what to do?

Silence.

I asked you, sergeant. Are you telling me what to do?

Ned I'm not, no.

Justin No, what?

Ned No, sir.

Justin We have important surveys to do this afternoon. I'll see you at the fort. (*He gathers his newspaper.*)

Dolly You'll be calling into the chapel, I'm sure, Justin. Maybe you should pray you'll stop turning into such a cruel little shit.

Justin Maybe you should just call into the chapel, Dolly. The one time only in the four years you're back home. I'd say you're the first Irish Catholic who lived in Italy and came back a heathen. Enjoy your dinner. I hope it chokes you, you selfish old bitch. You never listen to me. You never have.

> *He exits.*
>> *Esther wanders onto the shore and lights a cigarette.*
>> *Dolly goes out to join her.*
>> *Ned cuts more bread and eats.*

Rima Do you know what we'll do this afternoon, Anna? Dig up that gooseberry bush in Dolly's garden. I wish I'd done it forty years ago. Young ones put years on you, Ned. You're lucky not to have them.

Ned We still might.

Dolly What way is the army hardening Justin? What is he becoming? He was the gentlest boy. We were worried he was too soft. But I don't like this. He shouldn't have said that.

Esther And Ned should have stood up to him. But he won't. He never will.

Rima So Alec's back.

Dolly What would Ned like to eat this evening?

Esther Forget about Ned. That's not what you're thinking about.

Rima I wonder this time will he make a move.

Dolly Alec's my business, Esther, mind your own.

Esther Do you know what I'd like? Sail the Atlantic – swim across it. But I won't. You made the break and left, Dolly. I never did.

Dolly Much good it did me. Come in and eat, Esther.

Esther In a minute. I have my business to attend to.

Dolly goes back to the kitchen.
Esther stands smoking, listening to the sea.

Jesus – Jesus – Jesus.

The sound of the sea increases.

SCENE TWO

Dolly is ironing on the table.
Anna is sorting out dried laundry.
Ned is polishing a pair of boots that are already shining.

Anna You should be getting Mrs Horgan to clean your boots for you, sergeant.

Ned Some chance of that, eh Dolly?

Dolly smiles.

Anna If you were my man, I'd do it for you.

Ned You'll make someone a great wife, Anna.

Anna Everybody says that.

They continue working in a brief silence.

Will I run up the street and see if Mrs West and Mrs Horgan need a hand to carry down the messages?

Dolly You'll stroll up no street. Go and freshen up that room in case Mr Redding wants to stay the night.

Anna Right, Miss West. (*She leaves.*)

Ned How long since you saw Alec?

Dolly Four – five years ago – before the war. I've had the occasional letter from him. He stayed with me in Florence for about a month before he went on his wanderings. He was heading for Tibet.

Ned What the Christ would take him there?

Dolly Alec all over.

Ned Going out foreign – I don't know how yous do it. Even going into Derry, I feel like a stranger.

Dolly Don't let Justin hear that or he'll drum you out of the army. God, it's hard to imagine Alec in uniform, following orders. He was always his own man.

Ned Alec's not the kind of man to shirk his duty to his country.

Dolly He's spent more time out of England than in it. When we were at Trinity, he never took a holiday back there. Even Christmas he spent wandering through blizzards in the west of Ireland.

Ned You never came home when you were in Italy.

Dolly Too far to travel.

Ned Esther did it – to see you. All on her own. I couldn't face the journey. Do you miss it?

Dolly Funny what you miss. Smell of the bread. The taste of the water. The sky some nights, with a single star in it. The restaurant was going grand. Hard work, but I was learning all the time. Packed most nights. Every night. But I was always the Irishwoman, Ned. That was their nickname for me. The stranger. Even at the height of summer, the nights were cold. I used to take a hot-water bottle to bed with me always. Fill it in the kitchen, throw it over my shoulder, walk up the stairs. One night it burst scalding water down my back – I could barely walk. That was the night I turned the key to my door and came home.

Ned Why?

Dolly Bad luck. Evil. Mussolini and his boys. A sign. Scalding water. Run like hell, before hell catches you. You wouldn't want to know Italy, Ned, before the war.

Ned What are the Italians like?

Dolly The best. But they have a sad streak in them, and it's savage.

Ned Like ourselves.

Dolly No – they're not.

Ned Esther loved it.

Dolly She did when she came home. She didn't when she was there. The ever changeable Esther. For all the long years I've known my sister I still declare the woman to be a mystery. She's the one supposed to be like our father. If he'd lived longer, we might have known him better, and her. A mystery.

Ned She's hardly sleeping at all now. She's always walking on the shore.

Dolly She never slept much and she loves the water. You know that.

Ned She's talking to herself as well. I hope she's not getting a want in the head.

Dolly Nothing's wrong with the same one's head.

Ned She has nothing to do. You and Anna do all about the house.

Dolly Her job is to manage the money. That lady can make a pound go a very long way. She has every shopkeeper terrified.

Ned That part-time teaching job – she should never have stopped it.

Dolly She hated the school – truth to tell, she hated the children.

Ned No, she didn't. She did not.

Silence.

She did not hate the children.

Silence.
Alec has entered the herb garden, carrying a large bag.
He surveys the whole garden.

Dolly Ned, I've never said this, and I might regret it, but did you ever think of moving her out of this house?

Ned Into the married quarters at Dunree fort? You can't swing a cat in them. This is a grand big house. More than enough room. Your da, Dr West, left a fair whack of money. Esther's used to that way of living. What could I offer her?

Dolly Esther will be like our mother – getting worse with age, but that might make her better.

Ned You said she was like your father, and he did a runner, didn't he?

Silence

Dolly He came back.

Ned To die.

Dolly As good enough reason as any.

Alec speaks in an Irish accent.

Alec Excuse me, lady of the house, but would you have a cup of tea for a stranger?

Dolly The worst Irish accent in the world – Alec!

He comes to embrace her.
She has just been folding a shirt.
She presses it against him as they embrace.
She smells his shoulder.
He kisses her forehead.
She whispers.

Dolly I've missed you.

Alec Mutual.

He turns to Ned, who has his boot in his hand.
He goes to shake Ned's hand.
Ned drops the boot.
They shake hands and nearly embrace.

Alec Mr Horgan.

Ned Mr Redding. Rest your feet – sit down. Didn't you hear the man, Dolly West? He wants a cup of tea.

Dolly He'll get it.

Alec I think I can do better than tea, Mr Horgan – (*He produces a bottle of rum from the bag.*)

Ned Mr Redding, my favourite old grog. The bottle of rum. You remembered. Alec, you're as decent an eejit as ever looked over a half-door. Now I'm going to break your heart, bucko. I have to go to work. So I can't have one with you.

Alec But we will tonight, lad. We will tonight.

Ned I'd say we might, if we're let. Dolly West runs a very tight ship – who knows – after lights out and she's tucked up tight, who knows what badness might be afoot?

Dolly If you two boyos think you're in for a feed of drink without me in the middle of you, think again. Ned, off you go, and God save Ireland, said the heroes.

Ned God save Ireland, said the men.

Dolly You'll be poisoned talking to Alec before the evening's out.

Ned has pulled on his boots.
    He looks at his hands and then touches Alec's hands.

Ned Jesus, polish all over my hands. Did I get it on yours as well?

Alec Don't worry about it.

Ned I'll run them under the outside pump. Good luck, Alec.

Alec I'll see you, Ned.

They gently punch each other in the stomach.
    Ned exits.

Dolly I don't know what you do to Ned Horgan, but you always fill him with life. It's good to see you, Alec, you old rogue.

Alec Rogue – is that the best you can rise to?

Dolly You get no more. Those days are long gone. You think I was going to spend my days trailing after your favours to Tibet?

Alec Tibet – was that where I was going the last time? It was – yes. You were right not to trail me. I did have a romantic interlude there, in a manner of speaking.

Dolly You were going to marry a Tibetan? What would Mummy have said?

Alec Immediately onto marriage and mothers – Miss Dolly West. Anyway, we pitched camp in a quite remote area, and the natives were charming, very generous and welcoming. We were about to hit the sack, when this little girl – six or seven – she arrived with her yak. It was all decorated with bells and ribbons. We patted it and told her it was a lovely yak. She made it clear the yak expected more than patting.

Dolly She thought you were going to –

Alec Yes, with a yak.

Dolly You've had your fair share of dogs –

Alec That's enough. We got rid of her and the yak, or so we thought. She was back five minutes later with a younger yak that had no need of bells or ribbons. We sent that one packing as well, but I'm sure that somewhere in Tibet there's an ageing yak sipping gin with smeared lipstick thinking those bloody English turned me down for a younger model.

Dolly Jesus, I'm with the ageing yak.

Alec Dolly, you don't look a day over thirty – in yak years.

Dolly Watch it. You came home to join the army?

Alec I did. Quite a journey – some dicey moments – tell you about them later. I got home and signed up. My father wanted to land me a job in intelligence –

Dolly You never finished your degree in medicine, Alec –

Alec Don't be rude. I never wanted to, Dolly. I didn't want it, I was looking for danger – you know me – and I got it.

Dolly Danger? You're stationed in Derry, Alec.

Alec True, but I'm also nanny to a gang of extremely lively American boys, and while I can hit on many of our acquaintances who would think they had died and gone to heaven if they were in my position, the fresh smell of cock has not been to my liking since I was fifteen.

Dolly You had a fling with a man in your twenties.

Alec I was drunk.

Dolly It went on for three months.

Alec I was very drunk. I have not been similarly tempted. So I'm here to explain your ways to them. They have caused havoc wherever they have been posted.

Dolly Welcomed with open legs.

Alec And every other orifice. The powers that be saw I studied at Trinity College, presumed me to be a Dubliner, posted me here and I have to save them from the natives. Forgive me for using that word.

Dolly We are natives, Alec.

Alec Don't say that, Dolly – it doesn't sound terribly nice coming from you. Where is everybody? Where's your mad mother and your even madder sister? Where's the beautiful broth of a boy, Justin?

Dolly He's in the Irish army.

Alec Justin? Ten years ago he'd destined himself to the church. I thought he would be Pope by now.

Dolly He settled to be an officer in the Irish army. It came as no surprise. The child thrives on rules and regulations.

Alec Like yourself, Dolly. Number one rule – if you do something, do it perfectly. Number one regulation, don't do it for too long. Don't come back – unless it's to the old sod of Ireland.

Dolly For the duration of the war. I didn't fancy facing either side in Italy – yours or theirs.

Alec What happened to your restaurant?

Dolly Boarded up – hope it's still standing.

Alec The woman who couldn't boil an egg as a student –

Dolly We always had maids, we still do –

Alec And you call me a snob. Something for you. I raided Uncle Sam's pantry.

Dolly Alec, we're grand down here in the Republic. The rationing is not as severe as it is in the North. We have meat and butter –

Alec Not this. (*From his bag he produces two bottles of wine.*)

Dolly You'll be shot.

He produces two more.

I'll turn Protestant for you.

He produces two more.

I'm fetching you our yak, darling. (*She calls out.*) Anna, I want you – where are you?

Anna calls offstage.

Anna Hanging out clothes on the line. I'm finished – I'm coming. (*She rushes in with a large basket.*)

Dolly This is Mr Redding. This is Anna, who works for us. Anna Owens.

Alec You're much prettier than a yak, child.

Anna A what?

Alec Forgive my rudeness. How do you do?

They shake hands.

Anna My hands are all wet from the washing.

Dolly Put that wine in the basket.

Anna does so.

Break one and I'll break you. Run up the town and see your pals after that. Don't stuff yourself with fish and chips. You're eating good food here. Be back soon.

Anna I will, Miss West. Goodbye, sir. You didn't wear your uniform.

Alec No, I'm afraid I didn't.

Anna You look good in what you're wearing. Your shoes are lovely.

Alec You notice clothes – men's clothes?

Anna I notice the men wearing them. Does he think Irishwomen are stupid?

Alec I'm sorry I spoke.

Anna I didn't mean to be bad-mannered. Sorry.

Dolly Run on, Anna.

Anna exits, carrying the basket carefully.

Alec God, she sounds exactly like you when you first came to Dublin.

Dolly My accent hasn't changed that much.

Alec As much as you have, Dolly. She has the same cheek, that girl. You must breathe it in the air here.

Dolly Just as well – would you change us?

Esther rushes into the garden, shouting Dolly's name.

Jesus, what's wrong? Esther, has my mother had one of her turns? Is she all right?

Esther enters the kitchen.

Esther Your mother has not had a turn. Your mother has made a show of herself. She has shamed me for the last time. She is no longer any mother of mine. I disown her. (*She sees Alec.*) Alec, we were expecting you. Tell me, have I changed?

Alec No, Esther, you remain yourself.

Esther I'm only sorry you're here to see me murdering my mother, but at least you can say you saw me before I was hanged.

Alec What did she do to deserve being stretched by the neck until she's dead?

Esther I was arguing in the Co about the tea ration, she slipped away from me. I heard her muttering something about saying a prayer in the grotto. Our mother's grotto is nobody else's, Alec.

Alec It's the Crushkeen pub in the middle of the town. The snug. I remember.

Esther She's a glass to her lips, drinking when I walk in there, with two young American soldiers. My mother is getting drunk with two GIs. I'm not – she is. She has also invited them back here to eat with us. What's Justin going to say? You heard the outburst about Alec –

Alec Outburst?

Dolly Never mind.

Esther He doesn't want you in here because you're a British soldier now, Alec. I'm sorry –

Alec The shit.

Dolly Esther, your mouth –

Esther Should be cemented shut.

Anna Do you want me to leave?

Dolly You do, I'll leave with you.

>   *Rima, Marco and Jamie enter the herb garden. Marco and Jamie carry voluminous shopping bags.*

Alec If I am causing any offence whatsoever, I assure you –

Dolly Alec, stop acting the Englishman.

Rima Hello – guess who's here?

Esther They've guessed.

>   *Rima enters the kitchen.*

Rima Did you tell them about the boys?

Esther Don't you talk to me.

Rima They're strangers in a foreign land. They could be your own brother if he was fighting in the war. We're feeding them.

Esther They were feeding you with plenty of drink.

Rima I didn't have to put my hand into my pocket. Americans know how to treat their women. They are wee angels. Well, big angels, Dolly, you'll love them. They are gods. Gods of men. Young fellas, come in – come in.

>   *Marco and Jamie enter, still carrying the shopping bags.*

Dolly Hello, lads.

Marco Hi – hi.

Jamie nods.

Rima Leave down them bags and take your rest. You're as welcome as the flowers of May to dear old Donegal.

Marco Your sister must have told you who we were.

Esther I said nothing – how did you know she was my sister?

Marco Did you also tell her I hated you on sight?

Esther May I ask why?

Marco The way you dress.

Esther What's wrong with it?

Marco Nothing, if you're posing for the Statue of Liberty.

Esther I've never seen the Statue of Liberty.

Marco It shows, honey.

Esther I'm not your honey.

Marco My God, that woman's hair – was it suicide?

Esther My hair is my crowning glory.

Marco Did she say crowning or clowning? I have such trouble with consonants.

Esther I'm going to wring his neck.

Marco I am Marco Delavicario. This is my Irish-American cousin, Jamie O'Brien. We signed up together. Jamie brought the clothes he was standing in and a change of underwear. I brought one taffeta dress and a change of high heels. Who knows what might happen in the heat of the battle?

Esther They let a man like you into the US army?

Marco Right now they'd let a man like you into the US army.

Esther At least I'm a real woman.

Marco May God forgive reality.

Jamie Do the proper introductions.

Marco You must be Miss Dolly West.

He kisses Dolly's hand, as does Jamie.
Marco puts his arm around Jamie.

Marco Your mother has told us so much about you. Tell me it's lies.

Dolly Completely.

Marco looks into Jamie's eyes.

Marco I adore that woman already. I worship her mother. I hate her sister. She's all yours. Captain Redding, we know – from our briefing session about the natives.

Dolly You do call us natives?

Alec I may have cracked a joke –

Marco We all know each other – isn't this divine?

Rima Marco has great stories about the film stars. Do your Jean Harlow mouth, Marco.

He does so.

Did you hear the one about Jean Harlow and the cucumber? You get a dish of honey –

Dolly Mother, not in mixed company. Wait until the men have gone.

Rima Alec, it's yourself.

Alec It is, Mrs West.

Rima Rima to you, Alec.

Alec Good to see you, Rima.

Rima You're alive, Alec. May you stay so. Hard fight ahead, God protect you. Dolly, I've asked these boys to eat with us.

Dolly The more the merrier – we have enough.

Anna enters the kitchen.

You didn't stay long in the town, Anna.

Anna There was nobody there. I saw yous ahead of me. (*She looks to Jamie.*) You must be worn out carrying the shopping bags. (*She looks to Jamie.*) Will I make you all tea?

Marco That would be delightful.

Alec A cup of tea would be lovely.

Esther Do you know tea is rationed?

Marco You can count Jamie out from drinking tea. He's a coffee man.

Rima He'll wait a long time before he sees coffee in this country.

Dolly Does your cousin ever speak?

Marco I'll ask, shall I? Jamie, do you ever speak?

Jamie I would like a glass of water.

Anna I can fetch you some spring well water. Lovely and cold.

Esther Like himself.

Jamie smiles at her.

Jamie And like you.

Esther I think he speaks.

Justin enters from the shore. He eyes Alec coldly and nods. Alec returns the greeting.

Justin Alec.

Alec Justin.

Justin Am I to be introduced to the other gentlemen?

Dolly This is my brother. Mr Delavicario – Mr O'Brien – Justin West.

Justin A right gathering of the Allies.

Marco Boys together – that's right.

Justin You've crossed the border.

Marco Hasn't everyone?

Justin I beg your pardon.

Marco Just being chatty.

Justin I never am.

Marco You can use your tongue for other matters.

Justin Than what?

Marco Chatting.

Justin Yankee wit.

Marco Yankee wisdom.

From this exchange to the end of the scene, Justin does not take his eyes off Marco.
Anna gives Jamie a drink of water.
He downs it in one go.

Anna Isn't it lovely water?

Jamie Lovely. And cold.

Justin What are you doing in here – has the invasion begun?

Rima I invited them to eat with us. And they will – in my house, in my kitchen.

Justin Your kitchen? Are you sure, Ma? The word in the town is that this is Dolly West's kitchen. All soldiers welcome.

Dolly Whose word is that?

Justin Everybody's.

Dolly Then it must be right. So, welcome to you all. You'll eat tonight in Dolly West's kitchen.

Jamie Your beach looks very beautiful.

Esther It is beautiful.

Jamie Might we take a walk there?

Esther We might.

Justin I'll accompany my sister.

Marco I'll accompany my cousin.

Justin How courteous of you.

Marco Thank you, kind sir.

Anna Can I go for a walk, Miss West?

Dolly I need you to give me a hand.

Alec Let her, Dolly. Come along, Anna. I'll chaperone you. All these strong young fellows – I'll make sure you don't fall into temptation.

Anna Can I, Miss West?

Dolly Run on.

Anna takes Alec's arm.
They exit to the beach.
Jamie and Esther do likewise.

Marco I shall refuse your arm, young man. I do not trust men in uniform.

Justin What the hell are you?

Marco An angel fallen from the skies.

Justin Where exactly are you from?

Marco Paradise.

Marco exits.

Justin Is he not right in the head? Is there anybody in this house right in the head?

Rima I don't think so, son.

Justin exits.
Dolly and Rima look at each other.

I'm a bit tired. I'll have a wee rest before eating.

Dolly What are you doing, Ma?

Rima Me – doing what?

Dolly What have you brought into this house?

Rima Badness. Good, isn't it? A bit of badness.

SCENE THREE

It is evening, towards the end of supper, and wine is being drunk.

Dolly dishes out wild strawberries from a white bowl.

Anna serves them to the family and guests sitting around the table.

On the table there is a skeleton of a large salmon and the bare remains of a chicken.

There are also empty white vegetable dishes.

The bowls Anna serves are also white.

Marco helps Dolly and Anna serve and clear.

Alec opens wine. Ned opens bottles of Guinness.

Dolly Lemons – that's what I really miss, Alec. Gorgeous lemons. God, I love the smell of them. That's what these strawberries lack. Just a little taste of lemon juice. So forgive the dessert.

Alec It will be great, Dolly.

Ned I'd say this war could last for another ten years. It could, sir – it could.

Rima Don't say that, Ned – you'll wish it on us.

Ned I wish no such thing on this unfortunate earth.

Dolly Was the salmon all right?

Alec Perfect.

Rima Before the war I wouldn't have thanked you for fish. Now we have to eat it.

Marco approaches Ned.

Marco I don't believe we have been formally introduced.

Ned I don't believe so, no.

Marco My name's Mary – Mary O'Shaughnessy.

Ned That's very unusual.

Marco Yes, isn't it? But all the men in my family are called O'Shaughnessy. (*He walks off.*)

Justin And you think your people might have migrated from here to the States, O'Brien?

Jamie My father said his father came from Donegal, but I don't know where.

Rima I think you overcooked the chicken, Dolly.

Anna I did the chicken, Mrs West.

Rima Then it was grand, pet.

Dolly It was grand if she cooked it, but not if I did?

Rima I'm only encouraging the child. You can say nothing to that one.

Justin If you're a Donegal man, you're true Irish. Ancient Irish. Just off the coast about ten mile north of here there's a patch of rock they say was the earliest formation of the island of Ireland.

Rima Who says that?

Justin Geologists, Ma.

Rima Enlighten me what they do.

Justin They study the rocks and soils of a place and they discover what formations shaped a country like Ireland into being.

Rima Jesus, I could tell you that myself. Everybody knows that. A little bit of heaven fell from out the skies one day, and when the angels found it, it looked so lovely there they sprinkled it with gold dust and they called it Ireland.

Justin For God's sake, Mother.

Rima Don't for God's sake me. I'm not the one saying it. It's the song says it – I'm only repeating –

Esther And you believe everything you hear in a song?

Rima Well, I believe that from where I'm sitting it's a long way to Tipperary, it's a long, long way to go.

Esther Where did we dig her out of?

Rima Listen to that. Never finished her education. It's an old saying and a true one. Shite flies high when it's hit with a stick. Where's the pepper for these strawberries?

Marco Well, Jamie, are the Irish as you hope to find them?

Jamie No.

Rima Enlighten us why?

Jamie I thought you might dance and sing, and have the neighbours in to play music.

The Irish look at each other and then at Jamie.

Rima Son, if any neighbour crossed my door with his banjo, the next time he plays it it will be with his arse. Alec, you're being very quiet this evening. Mind you, he always was. I always liked Alec. There's one nice thing I'll say about the English: when they keep their mouths shut, they're grand.

Dolly And they wonder why the League of Nations never worked.

Rima I'm saying nothing against anybody. Alec's more than welcome. All nations welcome in this kitchen. Didn't I ask these two American boys to eat with us? And I'm glad I did, even if one seems to be deaf and dumb, and the other one is definitely wearing lipstick.

Marco Madam, I am an American soldier. I am most emphatically not wearing lipstick. A little rouge, yes. No Nazi's going to bitch about my bone structure.

Justin Do you know what the Nazis do to men like you?

Marco Why the fuck do you think I'm fighting them?

Silence.

Ned Is that why you're called Mary?

Esther Who's called Mary?

Marco Everybody, sister.

Rima What's it like with two men in the bed?

Silence. They all look at her.

I'm only asking. There was a man like that here. Nice chap. A baker. That was years ago. The word was he had the biggest micky ever seen on any man in this town. Thirteen inches. It gave a whole new meaning to the baker's dozen.

Silence.

Can I say nothing this night?

Marco Would someone pour me a very large whiskey very gently?

Justin does so.

Rima I was only saying –

Dolly We heard.

Rima I remember he was a Methodist. I suppose I'm not allowed to say that as well. Mind you, apart from him, I never had much time for the Methodists.

Justin Why not, Ma?

Rima What did they ever do to free Ireland? I have
nothing against Protestants as such. Then, I'm blessed.
I can recognise one immediately and watch my mouth.

Alec How would you recognise I was a Protestant?

Rima By your bicycle. If it has a basket, you're the other
side. They're always making chutney and giving it to
Catholics. If they didn't poison us with their free soup
during the Famine, they're going to do it now with their
pots of preserve. I'm still worried about this boy. Why
do you never speak?

Ned Me – sure I speak when I want to speak.

Rima Not you – I've been listening to you for years.
I meant him.

Ned I know – I was making a joke.

Jamie Mam, you talk a lot.

Rima I do.

Jamie I don't say much. Between the two of us, we say
what needs to be said. We're different. I like that. I don't
wear make-up. I don't like guys. Marco does. Let him.
I like difference.

Alec And you'll die fighting to prove it?

Jamie Yes.

Esther rises from the table and walks away.

Marco I love that boy. I'd marry him, but we're cousins.
We'd need papal dispensation. I'd still love to ask His
Holiness for that. It would be interesting to learn if the
Pope's vocabulary includes the expression, 'Who the fuck
is she?'

Esther
The King sits in Dunfermline Town,
Drinking the blood-red wine.

She is looking pensively into her wine glass.

Marco Is there more wine?

Justin pours Marco wine.

Rima Esther, don't sing. Dolly, don't let her. She knows sixty verses of 'The Green Glens of Antrim'.

Alec Marco, you're on whiskey. Don't mix the grape and the grain.

Esther Don't worry. I dislike singing. I prefer the deaf and the dumb.

Anna Lizzie the dumbie's back on holidays from the special school in Dublin. They do great things with them. She's learned Irish dancing.

Rima That will keep her in shoe leather.

Justin Are you going to do what he tells you?

Marco What?

Justin Not drink the wine I poured you? Are you going to follow his orders? You don't have to. You're a free man here. The British army have no power in this part of the country.

Alec I'm out of uniform tonight, Justin.

Justin To my eyes you are always in uniform.

Marco Stay out of this, Jamie.

Ned Justin, son, hold back like a good man.

Esther And turn out like you, Ned?

Ned There was a time it was good enough for you, Esther.

Esther Do you mind the time the cow shit lime and the monkey chewed tobacco?

Ned Have your say, Justin. The kitchen is yours.

Justin The kitchen's mine. The house is mine. And what's more, the port of Buncrana is mine. The ports of Ireland are ours, and ours alone. Look out there. That's what they want. The ports of our free neutral country. It is for them they want us in this war. They think they might still get us into it, because they believe – even after all they've done to us, all they've made us suffer, they still believe we could fear the Germans more than we hate the English. Alec, do you know how deeply you are hated?

Silence.

How deservedly you are hated?

Silence.

A bottle of rum, some wine – a drink over a table – so you think that will settle the difference between us? Have you no answer? Aren't you going to dazzle us with your British diplomacy? Or has that shit been scared out of you? What have you to face now? It's not a shower of Paddies with sticks and stones. It's the full might of Hitler's army. And you are going to lose the war. Germany will win the war. The might of Hitler's army will win the war.

Alec Then God help you, Justin, and you know why. God help all of us about this table. There are millions dying because of the might of Hitler's army. And their sacrifice might save your skin, but I call what they're suffering a damned sight worse than whatever you and your people have suffered. God save Ireland, isn't that one of your country's battle cries? Do you know who will save Ireland this time? English conscripts, Welsh miners, Scottish shipbuilders, Irish navvies – that's who'll save Ireland.

Justin Go to hell.

Alec When I go off to fight in this war, hell is where I'll be heading into. And Justin, you won't be with me.

Justin Don't call me a coward.

Marco He didn't.

Justin Because I'm not.

Marco He didn't call you a coward.

Justin I am not a coward, Marco.

Marco I know.

Justin exits to the shore and lights a cigarette.

Alec Will he be all right?

Dolly Follow him, Ned.

Ned No.

Jamie Marco.

Marco I need some air. Excuse me. (*He goes out to the shore.*)

Ned How are you boys going to get back to barracks? Derry's fourteen miles away. The last train's gone a while ago. It's a long hike.

Alec I've the car.

Ned Will they get into hot water?

Alec Not if I'm with them.

Ned I hope you don't think I'm speaking out of turn, Alec, but you boys do need to watch yourself in this town. Justin keeps the fight to words. Others here will use their fists and feet. Buncrana is not the safest of towns for you. Stay in Derry. Stay across the border.

On the shore Marco takes Justin's cigarette from his lips. He lights his own with it.

Marco I like your hatred. Don't lose your hatred.

Justin What would you know about it?

Marco Everything.

Justin What would you know about me?

Marco What you've told me.

Justin What have I told you?

Marco Everything.

Marco touches Justin's face. Justin kisses Marco's hands.

Justin You'll tell no one else?

Marco Come back to the house. After me. I'm there.

Esther Very kind of you, Ned. We can all be kind. I'm sure my mother and sister will welcome you in here whenever you're on leave. Dolly?

Marco enters.

Dolly They'll all be welcome.

Esther Mother?

Rima is asleep.

Mother?

Dolly Has she fallen asleep? Mother.

Rima wakes up.

Rima I must have nodded off. I'm getting old. Were there any fights?

Dolly Yes.

Rima I missed them. Any good?

Alec Yes.

Dolly Justin does love his country, Alec.

Alec So he must hate mine?

Dolly Sometimes he must, yes. In the years you lived here, did you not find that out?

Alec No, I didn't. I never will. Do you want to see Hitler win, Dolly?

Justin enters as the evening light turns to blue and gold.

Dolly Once a year when I was living in Florence, I took the train to Ravenna. I wanted to see the mosaics in the churches. They're from the sixth century.

Rima Something's older than myself.

Dolly Ma, you would have loved them. The colour, the life in them. When I looked up at the walls and ceilings, for the first time I knew what it was like to have breath taken out of your body at the beauty of what your eyes saw.

Rima What did you see, daughter?

Dolly A procession of men and women. They were white and blue and gold, walking towards their God, and it was the walking that was their glory, for that made them human, still in this life, this life that I believe in. I believe in Ravenna. I remember it. I came home to Ireland, so I could remember it – there would be one in this country who would not forget in case Ravenna is destroyed. I think it's my life's purpose to say I saw it.

Rima God spare it.

Dolly I think I know what yours is, Alec. It's to fight, to save us from Hitler. It's a great purpose. I hope you win. I'm frightened you'll die. I'm frightened you'll lose.

Alec God save Ireland.

The sea sounds.

Act Two

SCENE ONE

It is three months later.
  Rima is weeding in the garden, where she has placed
a chair.
  Anna is washing potatoes.
  Ned sits morosely in the kitchen.
  On the table there is a blue jug of milk, a slab of
butter and home-made bread.

Anna You don't play tennis yourself, Mr Horgan?

Ned Do I look as if I play tennis?

Anna Mrs Horgan loves it. Her and Mr Justin have a
match every good morning. When the boys come down
at weekends on leave, they play what's called doubles. It
must be great fun. They're always breaking their hearts
laughing when they come home. Mrs West says it's doing
Esther the power of good. The exercise has taken years
off her.

Ned Did you call my wife Esther?

Anna I meant no disrespect.

Ned She's Mrs Horgan to you and your like. Just
remember where you crawled into this house from. You
can be sent post-haste back there – if they'll have you.
Don't let yourself or this house down.

Anna I won't let them down and they won't send me
back to the convent.

Ned Then stop making sheep's eyes at that O'Brien fella.
I hope I haven't to remind you why you were reared in a

convent in the first place. It was the only place who would take you in. Your mother didn't want you. Your father didn't want her. Don't end up like that, Anna. You'll be barred from every decent house in this town.

Alec is by the shore.

Anna Maybe you should look to your own house.

Ned Do you want to feel the back of my hand?

Anna Could it be any harder than the back of the bitches' hands that reared me? Dear kind nuns? More like mad women. I am not afraid of the back of any man's hand. And maybe it's not me should be feeling yours.

Ned What are you saying?

Alec Good afternoon.

Ned Say nothing in front of the English stranger.

Alec enters the kitchen.

Alec I've just walked the five miles from Fahan. God, the White Strand. I do believe it's one of the great sights on this earth.

Ned You've seen a fair few of them, Alec.

Alec But it is truly magnificent on a clear day. When I was walking past the golf course at Lisfannon, I got it into my head, Neddy, we might play a few holes there.

Ned God, it's been years since I even set foot on the lower links.

Alec We hired a boat one year, Anna. We rowed from Fahan across to Fanad. Ned, Dolly, Esther, myself – the four of us. The sea – I'll never forget the blue.

Anna It must have been lovely.

Alec Like your eyes – that blue.

Ned We didn't hire the boat.

Alec Didn't we?

Ned It was my boat. Esther bought it for me as a birthday present. The first year we were married.

Alec How could I forget that? You were so proud of it. We joked about that. Ned's baby, that's what we christened it.

Ned We didn't. You christen a child, not a boat. You call a boat something. That's the correct word. You should know that, being English.

Alec I stand corrected. Apologies offered, old chap.

Alec salutes.

Ned Stop calling me that. I'm not old.

Alec I didn't mean –

Ned I'll take a walk round the shore front to see if these people are still at the tennis court.

Alec Will I stroll around with you?

Ned I can find my own way there. You don't have to lead me. Good day to you.

Ned leaves.

Alec What did I say to cause offence?

Anna How would I know?

Alec Were you two quarrelling when I came in?

Anna Why do you ask that?

Alec Well, your faces –

Anna I'm sorry our faces annoy you.

Alec Yours doesn't. It's a very pretty face.

Anna Pretty my arse.

Alec Anna, did I stumble on –

Anna Nothing – stumbled on nothing. What are you suggesting?

Alec I can say nothing right today. I don't seem to be saying what I mean. I did mean it about your eyes. There is the sea in them. Blue.

> *He touches her face.*
>   *He kisses her.*
>   *She laughs in his face.*

Anna You're an old man – old enough to be my father. (*She points at the dirty potato water.*) That's what you look like to me. Dirty. Not very pretty, am I? Not now.

Alec What's turned you sour like this?

Anna I was turned like this a long time ago. I know how to act sweet, but where's that getting me? I warn you – keep your hands to yourself. I'm no soft touch. I never was.

Rima Anna, would you fetch me a wee glass of milk?

Anna All right. Would you like a glass of milk as well?

> *He nods yes.*
>   *Anna pours a glass of milk and hurls it over Alec.*

There's your milk.

> *She pours another glass of milk and takes it out to Rima.*
>   *Alec towels his face with a dry dishcloth.*

223

Rima When is Dolly due back?

Anna She's late.

Rima She never had any notion of time. She wouldn't be caught by tides?

Anna She knows when they come in.

Rima This milk is nice.

Anna Lovely and cold.

Rima Like the Yank.

Anna I wouldn't know.

Rima You're growing into a fine woman. What you should do is get Dolly to teach you Italian. Go back there after the war's over.

Anna The war will never be over.

Rima Not for you – in this country. Too many long memories in Ireland. Leave it.

Anna You heard Ned's conversation –

Rima I hear everything. When I want to.

Anna Stop the weeding for today. You look tired. Will I sit and keep you company?

Rima You lazy wee bitch, get on and do your work. I know your like. We always had maids in this house. (*She gently pulls Anna to her and kisses her forehead.*) Good girl.

Anna What should I have said to Ned?

Rima What you did say.

> *Anna exits.*
> *Alec comes out to Rima.*

There's an awful smell of spilt milk. Have you been crying, Alec? Running after young ones – did you think she would takes years off you? Leave her to the Yanks. Make an honest woman of Dolly.

Alec She wouldn't take me.

Rima You haven't asked her.

Alec I know her answer.

Rima Isn't she wise then? Imagine being stuck with you making a pass after skirt that won't rise for you?

Alec Is that what happened to you and your husband?

Rima Who told you that – Dolly?

Alec I'm sorry – no – I shouldn't have –

Rima It was Ned then.

He nods his head.

That poor man's been dreading Esther will leave him since the day – hour they married.

Alec Will she?

Rima If she does she'll come back. Her father did. And he gave me a final gift – his son. That's why Justin is ten years younger than Dolly. He was always good at the giving – my man. Not just to me, but to all his fancy women. Still, there was enough to spare. I was left the house and a fair share of money. We were well off. Dolly could get to Trinity College –

Alec Where Catholics aren't supposed to go.

Rima Which is why she went. The same one was never Gospel greedy.

Alec Did he live to see his son Justin born?

Rima Just about. Sad that.

Alec Did Justin mind not having his father?

Rima Ask if I missed his father?

Alec Did you?

Rima I did, Alec.

Alec And you never –

Rima Strayed? No. When you give your heart and it's broken, you don't give it again. Well, I didn't anyway.

Alec Maybe I should make a pass at you, Rima?

Rima If I found a man's hand up my skirt now, I wouldn't know what he was looking for. Why don't you marry?

Alec My father – my mother –

Rima So?

Alec I didn't want to inflict the same unhappiness. Her crying like a lost child sitting on the bed beside me. Him walking the floor of their bedroom trying to make sense of what they'd done to each other. When she died, he kept on walking the floor – they should have separated long before they started living for the sole reason of hating each other. They kept on together – I'll never know why.

Rima We never know. I'll tell you a true story happened in this town. Two old women sitting drinking in a pub. In walked a beautiful young girl carrying a bunch of roses and wearing what looked like a brown dishcloth on her head. One old one – we'll call her Mary – she says, I swear to Christ that's the little flower, St Therese of Lisieux. The other one says, what would St Therese of Lisieux be doing in a pub in Buncrana? I swear it's her, Mary says. There's only way to find out, ask her. So Mary goes over and says to the young one with the dish cloth, Excuse me, myself and my friend was wondering if you are the little flower, St Therese of Lisieux? The young one looks up from under the dish cloth and says, Would you ever fuck off? Mary goes back and the friend says, Is it her? Is it St Therese of Lisieux? Mary says, I asked her if she was the little flower and she told me to fuck off. That's a pity, says the friend, now we'll never know.

Alec And that happened in this town?

Rima Well, it didn't happen in Moville.

Alec Poor Moville.

Rima Moville my bollocks.

Alec You don't have bollocks, Rima.

Rima You haven't put your hand up my skirt – caught you there.

Alec You're an honest woman, Rima.

Rima I'm a bad bitch that says what she likes. Give me an honest answer to this, Alec. How's the war going to shape?

Alec It's touch and go.

Rima Still? The Germans?

Alec Mad.

Rima The English?

Alec Angry.

Rima The Yanks?

Alec Savage.

Rima Are they savage enough?

Alec Yes, they are.

Silence.

Rima And the Jews?

Silence.

Is it as bad –

Alec It's worse, I think. We don't know –

Rima We do.

Silence.

If any country should have opened the door to any people facing what they are facing – Ireland –

Alec It might not be as bad –

Rima We did nothing to save them.

Alec Ireland's a neutral country.

Rima Do you believe that?

Alec No.

Rima Neither do I.

Alec Rima, you welcomed Marco and Jamie. You welcomed me, an Englishman –

Rima Into Dolly West's kitchen. It's her that feeds you. Don't thank me.

Alec You reared her.

Rima That's right. Blame me. The old horse.

Alec I'm praising you.

Rima I prefer money. Now give my head peace, Alec. I hear the delightful roaring of the young people. Ask Dolly to marry you.

Alec I know her answer.

Rima Then turn back to Anna. Enjoy your milk bath, Cleopatra.

Alec You are a bad bitch, Rima.

Rima May you die roaring for a priest, you English heathen. Ask Dolly to marry you.

> *Alec exits to the shore.*
> *There is a short silence.*
> *It is broken by the sound of birds.*
> *Rima stands and looks about her. She is suddenly very tired. She sits down again.*
> *Justin, Esther, Marco and Jamie enter. They are in tennis whites.*

Justin Christ, Ma, that was a great tennis match. You look tired. Are you all right? (*He kisses Rima.*)

Rima What was the score?

Justin First set, six–four to us. Second set, six–two to them. Third set, Esther, my, dear?

Esther Ten–eight, to us.

Justin I really thought I was going to go under. I got the racket in my hand and I played like a lunatic. No man was going to beat me. Ma, I wish you were there.

Rima And the score was?

Justin Ten–eight, yes. Ma, we were mighty. You should have seen us.

Esther I haven't a spark of breath left. They've killed me.

Justin Ten–eight, third set. Serving down the line, excellent advice, Esther.

Esther I'm going to die, Ma.

Justin We beat the Americans. We beat the Yanks, Esther. And they can really play, Ma. (*He lifts Rima into the air.*) Two hundred million of them – the best army on God's earth – and the Irish beat them.

Marco To punish myself I think I shall break a nail.

Justin Are yous starving? Do you want to eat before we swim?

Esther He wants to swim?

Marco He wants to eat?

Rima Dolly's left some bread and milk for you. Justin, son, swim and then eat.

Justin Come on, we'll hit the water, then we'll tackle the grub. (*He exits to the shore.*)

Marco Tennis, swimming, drill practice, dormitories – and to think my mother reared me to hate men. Tell me, do you think this kind of life is affecting me?

> *Marco grabs a tennis racket.*
> *He marches and expertly performs rifle drill with the racket.*
> *He suddenly drops the racket and shrieks.*

Don't look at me – don't look at me. (*He races off to the shore.*)

Rima When I met that young fella first, I thought he was mad. Now I think he's from somewhere on Mars.

Jamie Manhattan actually.

Rima God help Manhattan. Are they all like him? How did they let him live in New York?

Jamie By the expert use of his fist and feet. And he was well taught.

Esther Who by?

Jamie Me – the day I beat the shit out of him. Tough love. Learn to fight or die.

Rima Savage.

Jamie I had to be.

Rima Good.

Esther Aren't you the hard man?

Jamie When I have to be.

Esther And when you don't?

Jamie I'm not telling.

Rima Thank God for the good summer. It's not always that warm here. And the winters in Donegal are rough.

Jamie Not as rough as winter in New York. I like that time of year. You'd love the city then, Esther. We could skate together.

Esther I don't think I'd be too safe on the ice.

Jamie You would be with me. (*He takes her in his arms, dances with her, lifting her high into the air.*) See – you didn't fall. You were safe.

Esther I suppose so.

Jamie Come on, Esther, let's go for a swim. The water will be beautiful. Cold.

Esther Now I'm to do as you tell me?

Jamie If it makes you happy.

Esther Well, Ma, will I go for a swim?

Rima Stay here and keep me company. I've been on my own all day.

Esther The boss has spoken, Jamie.

Jamie All right. Good afternoon, ladies.

Rima God bless.

Jamie exits to the shore. Anna is waiting for him. Esther walks about the garden. Rima is looking silently into the garden.

Anna Are you going for a walk along the shore?

Jamie I guess I am, Anna.

Anna You're always saying we should go for a walk.

Jamie I am?

Anna You know you are, God forgive you. What about today?

Jamie If you like.

Anna I like.

She gives him her arm and they walk together. Esther leaves down the newspaper.

Esther Ma, what do you think has come over Justin? Do you remember even as a child he would nearly faint if anyone saw him in his drawers? Now every chance he gets, he's never out of those baggy shorts. What's happened to him?

Silence.

I'm asking you what's happened to him?

Rima I'm sorry, I wasn't listening to you. I was looking at that patch in the garden where we grew pansies before the war. I always loved to look at them. They have magnificent colours.

Silence.

Ned was looking for you.

Esther He knew where I was.

Rima He knew who you were with.

   Silence.

I said he knew who you were with.

Esther I'm sorry, I wasn't listening to you. I was looking at that patch in the garden where the piss-the-beds grew before the war. I never liked to look at them. They were useless to man or woman.

   Silence.

I'm going in to read the papers.

Rima Maybe Justin's wearing shorts because somebody told him he had nice legs. Don't worry – it wasn't Jamie.

Esther Jamie?

Rima I meant to say Ned. So you're safe enough.

Esther I always will be.

   She goes into the kitchen to read the paper.
   Dolly enters pushing a wheelbarrow of mackerel and mussels.

Rima Jesus Christ, it's Molly Malone. (*She sings.*) Crying cockles and mussels alive – alive o.

Dolly It was the only way to haul all this home. We have a houseful for the dinner tonight. I've mussels to start with, then there's mackerel.

Rima Is it only fish to eat? I think I'm turning into a mermaid. My arse will grow a tail soon.

Dolly It's good for you, mackerel.

Rima So's a beautiful big black man and I'm not seeing many of them.

Dolly I'll do my best to find you one.

Rima Do you know a man in Urris married a mermaid?

Dolly Urris men would marry anything.

Rima Don't you run down Urris. This man caught the mermaid in his nets. She granted him one wish. He wished she would grow legs, and they did grow long and beautiful on her. He took her ashore and he married her. They lived happily for a year and a day till their baby was born. Then she went back to the water with the human child and was never seen again. You see, he'd been tricked. She had caught him, not him her. So the Urris people believed. They have their own way. Very smart people, your father used to say. He loved Urris. Did all his fishing there. That man should never have been a doctor. He should never have come from money. Fishing – that's what he wanted to do. Your grandfather wouldn't hear of a son of his roughing it on a boat. But he loved the water. He knew Lough Swilly like the back of his hand.

Dolly I didn't know him, Ma. He left just after I was born. I didn't like him when he came back, and he died before I had time to change my mind.

Rima You're very hard on him.

Dolly Why did you marry my father, Ma?

Rima You better get these fish inside. They'll turn –

Dolly Why did you marry him? Why did you marry my father?

Rima You'd be better off asking why did he marry me. I was the blacksmith's daughter. Your grandfather wasn't too fond of that. He looked down his nose at the whole town. Your da, Paddy West, had bowed to him over the fishing. He didn't bow a second time. So we married and he tried his best to settle. But I was not the woman who should have been your father's wife. None of the others were either. Maybe your da should have married a mermaid, who would have left him after a year and a day.

Dolly But he came back to you, Ma.

Rima He came back to me, I saw his remorse. I said to myself, but not to him, too little, too late. That's changed. I forgive him now. And I forgive myself for what happened. What did happen? We had three children. Three good children. I love you all. You love me. Take care of each other.

Dolly What's brought this on?

Rima The lack of drink. Get in and fetch me a small whiskey. When I say small, I mean my small, not your small.

Dolly You want a large whiskey – just say what you mean.

Rima I say what I mean.

Dolly Do you want water in it?

Rima I do not, and I don't want herbs in it either.

Dolly You're getting herbs on your mackerel, like it or lump it.

Rima I'd love a bit of dulse from Urris. God, I can taste the salt. I'd love somebody would give me one wish. Do you know what I would be, Dolly? A big seabird.

Dolly Are you sure you need this whiskey?

Rima I'd spread my white wings and I'd fly all over the world, China and India, starting here in Buncrana and then up to Malin Head, and I'd never touch the soil of Ireland again until I travelled the whole earth, landing back again in my own garden.

Dolly If you ever wondered why none of us were right in the head, just listen to yourself. (*She goes into the kitchen.*) Anything good in the paper?

Esther De Valera shit himself. What are you doing?

Dolly Pouring herself a whiskey.

Esther She's starting early.

Dolly Where is everybody?

Esther The boys are up swimming.

Dolly Is Alec with the lads?

Esther He might be.

Dolly Is Ned up with them?

Esther Why are you so worried about Ned?

Dolly I'm not.

Esther Neither am I.

   Silence.

Mind your own business, Dolly.

Dolly Mind yours, Esther.

Esther Deliver the drink to the Queen of Sheba.

   Dolly goes out to the garden.

Dolly Mammy, here's your whiskey.

   Silence.

Ma, are you all right – are you sleeping?

Silence. She touches Rima.

Mamma.

The glass of whiskey falls from her hands. Silence.

Esther.

Dolly enters the kitchen. She grabs Esther's hands.
A wail comes from Esther.
Darkness.

Blue.
The closed coffin.
Esther, Dolly and Anna stand in mourning. Alec, in
a black suit, stands by them.
Justin, Ned, Marco and Jamie are in uniform.
The soldiers carry the coffin. The women and Alec
follow it.

SCENE TWO

A seascape and shore.
It is evening, with signs of a storm mounting.
Justin and Marco are lying together.

Marco You can cry if you want to.

Justin I can't. If I start, I won't stop.

Marco takes his hand. Justin lets it go.

Not outside.

Silence.

Marco She knew you loved her.

Justin She knew I mocked her.

Marco She knew more. She knew about me and you.

Justin Did it kill her?

Marco No, it didn't.

Silence.

I don't have much time left in Derry. We're going to be fighting in Europe soon. Do you want me to go?

Justin I don't want you to die.

Marco Do you want me to go?

Justin In the evening that's in it, my mother's died, let me be, please, love.

Marco Love?

Justin Yes.

Marco Thank you.

Justin Thank you. What was I like before I met you? Twisted, miserable git. I'm so ashamed –

Marco Shut up about your shame.

Justin But what was I like?

Marco A Catholic bigot.

Justin Not all Catholics are bigots.

Marco They are where we're concerned.

Justin I once went to confession. I told this priest about myself. I was nearly shitting myself, Marco.

Marco Thank you for sharing that with me.

Justin The point is – he was a young priest, about my age. I think he believed I was trying to – you know. He started to tell me how much he loved women. How he'd

love to get married. He went on and on. He wanted me
to forgive him, because he couldn't help me. And I
wanted to, but I couldn't, because I wanted –

Marco All I want from the Catholic church is an apology.
A long apology. And I hope they will understand when
I refuse to accept it.

Justin Too little, too late – my mother's old saying.

Marco She also used to say I was from Mars. I liked
that. It showed she knew exactly what I was. And what
was I like before I met you?

Justin Very smart, funny, a bit scary –

Marco A bit? I do not think so. Very scary. Twisted,
mean cissy queen.

Justin Don't call yourself that.

Marco It's what my father called me every day until
I kicked myself out of his house. I tried to live up to it.

Justin And your mother?

Marco Our Lady of Second Avenue? She once found
some sketches I'd done of dresses when I was seven years
old. She poured ketchup on every page, salt and lots
of pepper. She made me eat them one by one until I
vomited. I thought it was blood, the red coming up my
throat.

Justin And you were a seven –

Marco – year-old cissy.

Justin You were a seven-year-old child.

Marco I hate her. I hate him. My mother. My father.
Don't lose your hatred? Remember. I'm fighting this war
because of hatred.

Justin And if you win, what happens then – what happens – do you stop hating? What difference –

Marco This difference. I will be able to look into the face of every man who fights beside me, and I will be able to say that in this war we fought on the same side against Hitler. Now you are fighting on Hitler's side because of your hatred of me and my kind.

Justin So your hatred of them will save you during this war?

Marco Don't lose your hatred. I told you. Hatred brought me to you.

Justin And only that?

Marco I'm the man from Mars, for God's sake. The loneliest man on the planet. I thought, till I met you. You were even lonelier. So I had to love you.

Justin kisses Marco.

Please, not here – not outside. Not when nobody's watching.

Justin I don't want you to go.

Marco When I come back, could we live in Italy?

Justin Jesus, yes. I'd love that. I've a bit of money from my father. Yes, Marco, yes. Dolly can teach me Italian. You're on. Where – what part of Italy?

Marco The Bronx?

Justin That's in New York.

Marco You poor boy, geography will be the death of you.

Justin Marco, you're to come home safe.

Marco Justin, I'm very frightened.

Silence.

Justin You're to come home to me.

Marco I will, yes. (*He kisses Justin's hand.*)

Ned (*offstage*) Wait, Dolly. Will you wait for me?

Justin Twisted mean cissy queen.

Marco And you love it.

They exit running.
Dolly enters, furious, followed by Ned.
The sky is darkening.

Ned Dolly! Dolly!

Dolly Keep that wife of yours away from me, or I'll swing this night for my sister if I see any more tears from her. That self-centred bitch is making so much mileage out of her grief, I'm beginning to wonder if she wanted my mother to die.

Ned Dolly, funerals are a funny business. They're worse than weddings. Families fight.

Dolly Put manners on that woman for once in your life, Ned, or I will – and it will be a sorry sight. In all the years I've come home, I've held my tongue about that bitch –

Ned My wife is a good woman.

Dolly You poor fool.

Ned Not where Esther's concerned.

Dolly Fool.

Ned I won't let you talk to me like that.

Dolly From me you'll hear the truth, Ned.

Ned You're saying what everybody's saying. Do you think I'm deaf –

Dolly Deaf and blind.

Ned I know the truth about me and Esther. Rima knew as well –

Dolly Rima took that young Yank into the house, and she knew what she was doing.

Ned Rima would never – to me – if I were to pray to her – in heaven –

Silence.

She loved me.

Dolly And to prove it she set you up to see if you were man enough –

Ned Man enough – dare any woman in this house doubt if I'm man enough? Do you know about your brother –

Dolly And the American soldier I hope he's fucking? We know. Rima knew. She set that up as well. That's what she wanted. Stop saying prayers to that woman. She'd spit in your face rather than receive them. She believed in this world, not the next. She believed, God help us, in the three she's reared, and what have her two brave daughters done to honour her? One's barren because she couldn't tell the man she wanted that she did want him. And the other is barren –

Esther and Alec enter.

Ned Stop this chat.

Dolly Barren.

Esther Roar it louder, Dolly West. Let the whole town hear you.

Dolly The whole town knows it, Esther. What do you think they were whispering at the wake? When you were shaking their hands and crying in their arms, what were they saying behind our backs?

Esther I happen to think better of people –

Dolly You always have been a liar.

Esther The truth's coming out now.

Dolly You have always run rings around people and got away with everything, the way you did to my father.

Esther Back to that old jealousy.

Dolly You couldn't run rings around me or my mother.

Esther I've never tried that with anybody.

Dolly Then what are you doing to him – to Ned?

Alec Dolly, you'll regret –

Esther Regret what?

Dolly What do you think that young fella sees in you?

Esther What young fella?

Dolly Do I have to spell it out?

Esther Spell away. I've nothing to hide.

Ned She has nothing to hide – swear to God.

Dolly He sees a soft touch, a woman ripe for picking, an old woman.

Esther Stop it – make her stop it, Ned.

Ned Dolly, I'm warning you.

Dolly Daddy's girl has grown up into an old woman

Silence.

A sorry old woman. A foolish old woman. And in that she is like her sister.

Silence.

Esther I'll tell you what he sees in me.

Ned Stop, Esther, you're breaking my heart.

Esther He sees someone who cares if he lives or dies –

Ned I care about you.

Esther He sees someone he can make happy.

Ned Stop.

Esther He sees a woman whose heart and head have not grown too hard to say to him the kind of things you have said to me this night.

Ned Your good heart, Esther, would never let you say things like that to her.

Esther And I could, Ned. I know all about that – whore. And he as well – Alec knows – her whore master. But I never have, Dolly. And I have always told you the truth, Ned. I'm no liar.

Ned Esther, if you leave me, I may as well walk into the water.

Esther He's asked me. I've said no. Every night Jamie's down here he asks to meet me by the water. I say I might. God forgive me, Ned, I do say I might. But I never have. I never will. I won't leave you, Ned. Take me home. Take me out of that witch's sight.

Ned Dolly, fuck off out of our lives.

Esther The first time you said fuck, Ned. You know what to do.

Ned leads Esther off.

Alec What do you think you were doing?

Dolly Finishing what Rima West set in motion.

Alec Your mother –

Dolly Is at peace now. How do you like the Irish at war, Alec? We have a genius for it, but only when it's confined to our own. To save my family from destroying itself, you do not know what I would do. And if you want to stretch a point, you love your country and I do mine, as I love you, but if you and your allies invade Ireland, I will be the first to put a bullet through your brain.

Alec Really? Well, we'd better not then. I won't anyway. I'm quite fond of my brain. Dear old noggin.

Dolly Are you trying to be funny?

Alec No – not funny. More amusing really. What the French call *amusant*. I'm sure the Italians have a word for it. Do tell me. By the way, you said you loved me.

Dolly I did not. I said I loved my country.

Alec And me. You love me. I distinctly heard you.

Dolly Alec, give my head peace. I've just buried my mother and lost my sister for life. Everything is gone. Even the restaurant in Italy is probably bombed to the ground. Just give my head peace.

Alec Dolly, why did you go to Italy? Why did you leave me?

Silence.

Dolly I left before you could leave, as you would have.

Alec Did you miss Rima there?

Dolly I missed you.

Silence broken by Dolly's sobbing, which she quickly stops.

What will I do if you die in this war?

Alec You'll find out soon.

Dolly It's happening – you're heading off to fight?

He nods.

So it's happening – the invasion?

Silence.

Ask me something.

Silence.

Ask me.

Silence.

Alec If I ever asked you to marry me, you would run a mile.

Dolly I'm standing still, Alec.

He takes Dolly's hand. He moves it through his legs, up to both his breasts.
He kisses her hand.

Tell me what you need. Woman or man?

Alec Both.

Dolly You can have both in me. (*She kisses him violently.*)

Alec What will I do if you die in this war?

Dolly You'll find out soon.

Alec Tonight.

Dolly This night.

Light fades on Alec and Dolly.
  There is thunder.
  Jamie comes from the darkness. He drinks from a
bottle of whiskey.
  Anna also appears from the darkness.

Anna Honest to God, old ones – wouldn't they turn
your stomach?

Jamie takes a slug from the bottle.

I might have a mouthful of that, if you'll let me.

He hands her the bottle. She drinks and chokes.

Is this gin?

Jamie Whiskey.

Anna I only drink gin.

Jamie You don't drink at all, Anna. Why tell lies? I don't
like lies.

Anna She's a liar, Esther Horgan is. Why blame me?
Why want her? She's a married woman.

Jamie I don't any more.

Anna Wise man, stay away from married women.

Jamie And you should stay away from married men.

Anna You dirty beast – you're not.

Jamie Smart girl – I'm not.

Anna Why say you were and scare the daylights out of
me?

Jamie Would it stop you if I were married, Anna?

Anna No, Jamie, it wouldn't. I would do anything for you. I'm dying about you.

Jamie Thanks, pal. Thanks. I've seen a man die. He was fighting for breath. Fighting for his life. He was my father.

Anna I never knew who my father was.

Jamie I didn't either. He didn't let me. But he held my hand when he was dying. I can't forget him breathing. Trying to say my name. I was called after him. Jamie. He smelt like death. Jamie. A smell of shit. And honey, the shit's scared out of me. I know I'm going to die. I'm going to die.

He begins to cry softly.

Anna I want to help you. Let me.

She slips off her dress.

Show me how to help you. You're going to live, Jamie. You're going to live.

They lie down together.
The storm erupts.
The sky starts to clear of the clouds' disturbance.

Act Three

Church bells.
  Suitcases and kit bags are packed, ready to go.
  Ned enters pushing a pram.
  In the kitchen Esther bastes a leg of lamb that is
nearly done.

Ned
  And the sultan of Byzantium is laughing as they run,
  There is laughter in those fountains in the face of all
      men feared – the face of all men feared –

  He pauses.

How does the rest of that poem go, daughter dear? 'The
Battle of Lepanto.' We won that, and the West was saved.
Somewhere near Venice. That's where Lepanto is. One
day we'll go to Venice, pet, and walk on the water. We'll
see the moon in the sky with one star beside it.

  Dolly enters the kitchen.

Dolly That smells good.

Esther You think it's alright?

Dolly It is.

Esther Did you look in on Justin and Marco?

Dolly Sleeping with their arms around each other. Justin
was crying in his sleep, Esther.

Esther Jesus, Dolly.

Dolly Do you remember the day he was born? Mammy
was out in the garden planting flowers, when her waters

broke, and she roared at the top of her voice, I have a son, I know it's a son.

Esther And it was. Daddy had come home.

Dolly Mammy was happy.

Silence.

Dolly Esther –

Esther Forgiven. Forgotten.

Silence.

Dolly Will you be lonely without us?

Esther I was always lonely here.

Silence

Esther Is Alec still down by the shore? Has he talked much yet?

Dolly shrugs.

Esther Maybe he'll talk to you in Italy.

Dolly I'll see if he wants a walk.

Dolly goes out to Alec.

Ned
There is laughter in those fountains in the face of all
    men feared,
It stirs the forest darkness, the darkness of his beard.
It curbs the blood red crescent, the crescent of his lips,
For the inmost sea of all the earth is shaken with his
    ships.

Unnoticed by Ned, Esther enters the garden.

Ned We've won. We've beaten them. Destroyed Hitler. May you never know his like. Dear girl, never know what we have known these past six years. Never have to fight the Battle of Lepanto.

Esther Never have to learn it – it's a rotten poem. What else are you whispering to the child?

Ned Baby talk – nonsense.

Esther You better practise it, Ned. The men home from the war – that's all you can say to them.

Ned They're like children, Esther. They've had a bad dream. We have to comfort them.

Esther Wee Patricia is all right?

Ned Grand.

He pushes the pram towards her. She pushes it back.

Esther Take the baby for a walk by the shore, Ned.

Ned Good sea air, good for her lungs.

Esther Perfect for her lungs.

Ned Perfect – isn't she?

Esther She is.

Ned I love her the way I love you.

Esther Stop.

Ned Irishmen are no good at compliments.

Esther They're not.

Ned Compliment – yes. Esther, do you remember how I asked you to marry me? I was too nervous to say it out straight, so I wrote to you: Would you do me the greatest compliment any woman could do to a man? You said yes. But I spelt it c-o-m-p-l-e-m-e-n-t. You told me to spell it right. I always learn from you.

Esther You do, Ned.

Ned I'll take the baby for a walk.

He goes off to the shore and exits.
   *Justin enters in his underwear, his trousers over his
arm.*

Justin Jesus, that man loves you.

Esther He does, yes. He does indeed. Would you put
your trousers on in front of a lady?

He does so.

How's Marco?

Justin All right. Not great.

Esther Jesus, this war has changed us all. What are we
now, Justin?

Justin Managing. Aren't we?

Esther Managing, that's the best we could ask for. I had
married the best of men. I didn't love him, I still don't.
But he is still the best of men. You can't wait to get away.

Justin The house is all yours.

Esther It was left to the three of us. I'll keep it safe. For
you and Dolly – to visit when you like. You'll get a great
tan in Italy. I might not know you if you come back. You
might not know me.

Justin Have you seen Jamie?

She shakes her head.

Esther He hasn't come down.

Justin Maybe he won't.

Esther That would be all right.

Marco enters, in pyjamas, agitated.

Marco Where were you?

Justin I haven't left the house.

Marco You said you would stay with me while I was sleeping. I woke up and you're not there.

Justin Marco, this is driving me stone mad. You're expecting me to watch over you twenty-four hours a day.

Marco I want to see you beside me. I don't want you to die.

Justin I'm not going to. The war's over. For Christ's sake it's over. The war is over.

Esther Marco, you're in Ireland. You're safe. You've had a bad dream –

Marco What I saw was no dream, lady. I know what I've seen. Justin, tell her.

Justin Esther, leave us. Just leave us.

Esther exits.

Marco What did that bitch mean? Dreams? The fucker – fucker.

Justin She's my sister.

Marco She didn't have to face what I had to face. I hate –

Justin Hate, you are full of it. You hate women, you hate men who love women –

Marco I fought better than any straight man.

Justin You fought the same as any straight man.

Silence.

Marco I saw the dead, Justin. I saw the dead stretched like sheets of paper on the shore. White as paper. All dead. I have to vomit. Red sauce. All over the dead.

Justin It's blood, Marco.

Marco It's not.

Justin This time it was blood, red – red blood.

Marco All my dreams are red.

Justin Then you're going to have to stop dreaming. Because I will not live like this. I will not be your nursemaid in Italy. I know how hard it's going to be to manage there, and if we're going to survive together, then you will pull your own weight.

Marco The way you did during the war, Justin, holding the fort back in dear old Ireland. You always knew you were safe so you let us suffer for you. If I'm full of hate, you and the Irish, you're full of shit. Shit.

Justin smashes his hand across Marco's mouth.

Justin The next time you open your dirty mouth, you apologise to me. You apologise. I have spent over a year not knowing anything about you. And to bring you home I would have done anything a man dared have done – I swear that. You talk about your dreams, Marco. What about mine? My dreams were full of you. Am I not the right fool? You want to run back to New York, to Mammy and Daddy, and show them the cissy son is the suffering, conquering hero, and all will be forgiven. Run on back. Good luck. May all your dreams be red.

Silence.

Marco That fucking colour never suited me.

Silence.

Justin You can wear anything.

They embrace.

Marco So we're going to Italy?

Justin Hold me back.

Marco Am I that full of hate?

Justin When you want to be.

Marco When I need to be. But not all the time?

Justin Not all the time.

Marco Justin, don't hit me again.

Justin I won't.

Marco Unless I tell you.

Jamie enters the kitchen.

Justin Is Anna not with you?

Jamie She's showing off her ring to some girls she knows.

Marco And the proud fiancé is not by her side?

Jamie I can't take the screams of joy.

Marco Come on, smile, Jamie – you're going to marry the girl.

Jamie And I'm sure my queer cousin wishes us well.

Marco I do.

Jamie And you, Justin, our good fairy?

Justin Anna deserves all the luck in the world.

Jamie And she'll get that from me?

Justin She'll make you happy.

Jamie Yeah. Esther about?

Justin She was here a minute ago.

Jamie I'll wait for her.

Justin Ned and Esther are trying –

Ned enters the garden with the pram.

Jamie I need to talk to her.

Marco Justin, let him. It has to be done. Come on. I do want you to be happy, Jamie. Don't call Justin your good fairy. He's mine. And do not call me your queer cousin. The way the war's aged you. I look young enough to be your daughter. Ciao.

Marco and Justin exit.
    Jamie lights a cigarette and enters the garden.

Jamie Look who's back, buddy boy.

Ned I can see for myself.

Jamie Why do I get the idea you're not pleased to see me?

Ned You tell me. Yanks know everything.

Jamie We knew how to win a war rather than sit on the sidelines shitting ourselves.

Ned My arse is clean.

Jamie Who wiped it for you?

Ned I'll wipe you, boy, once and for all.

Ned flattens Jamie.

Get up. I've not finished with you yet.

Jamie grabs Ned.
    They fight fiercely, destroying the garden.

Esther rushes into the fight, fearing neither.

Esther What are you doing? Stop this – stop it now.

The fight stops at Esther's intervention.

What are the two of you playing at?

Jamie He's defending your virtue, Esther. We're fighting over you. (*He laughs.*) Christ, look at what we're fighting over. Is she worth it, Ned? She's already turned into the bitter old bitch she deserves to be. On the streets of New York she couldn't give it away.

Ned I've given you a fair warning –

Esther I'll settle this. Not you. Get the child away.

Ned Tell him that it's my child. Tell him. It is my child, isn't it?

Jamie A bit of doubt, eh Ned boy?

Silence.

Ned Tell him. Tell me.

Esther That is my child.

Ned And mine – is it mine?

Esther You tell him, Jamie.

Silence.

Tell him the truth.

Jamie The child's yours.

Ned Will you get out of our lives now, O'Brien? Will you go back to your own country?

He exits to the garden, looks at the pram, and tries to walk away from it but can't.
He pushes the pram out.

Jamie Do you know what you've done?

Esther You've got Anna.

Jamie Leave her out of this. You're looking as though you hate me. Do you? Do you hate men?

Esther I don't think much of most of them.

Jamie You marry a man you despise. You pretend to want me, I fall for it and you –

Esther Walk away. Back to where I started.

Jamie Why?

Esther I'm my father's daughter. We tend to leave people we love.

Jamie You love me?

Esther Yes. But I've lost you. And you've lost me. That's why you want me. That's what hurts you.

Jamie And that's what you enjoy.

Esther No, Jamie. You haven't been listening to me. If you had, you would have heard my heart breaking.

Jamie Esther –

Esther I know what I'm doing. I know what's for the best.

    Anna enters from the garden.

And here's the best girl you could get. Anna pet, have you been up the town showing off your sparkler? Let me see it again. It is a beautiful ring.

Anna Everybody says it's the last word.

Esther Congratulations again, to you both.

Anna Thanks, Mrs Horgan.

Esther Less of the Mrs Horgan. You don't work for us any more. It's Esther you call me now. And you've to promise to write from America.

Anna I will, Esther, and I promise to sign it Mrs Jamie O'Brien. (*She laughs.*) It still sounds wild funny. I'll never get used to it.

Esther You will. We all do. I've a dinner to put on the table. We'll eat soon. Thank God that sister of mine's taught me about cooking. If she hadn't, my husband might starve to death.

Anna Where is Miss West – Dolly? I want her to see the ring.

Esther Out walking the town with Alec.

Anna Is he ever going to get better? Will he ever talk to anybody again?

Esther He talks to Dolly. He'll talk to us all in time. (*She exits.*)

Anna Jamie, thank Christ the war didn't drive you mad.

Jamie I had you to come home to.

Anna Me? You had her to come home to. So, she's turned you down. Think I don't know? Well, I'm not proud. I'll take her leavings. You're worth having. (*She kisses him.*) You like them tough, don't you? You think she's tough. I'm tougher. I've had to be. Now, will I enjoy New York?

Jamie You were made for each other.

Anna Just like us.

Jamie You think so?

Anna I know so.

Jamie And if we turn into Esther and Ned?

Anna We'll say a little prayer that we won't. I really want to say a prayer. A quick trip to the chapel. It will be the last time I'll see it. I will never, ever come back here. And neither will you. I'll see to that.

> *Jamie and Anna exit.*
> *The kitchen goes into half-light.*
> *Alec and Dolly enter the shore.*

Dolly Alec, I can't live in England. Why are you asking me to do that? There's better ways of leaving me, man.

Alec I have to live there.

Dolly You've never settled there before. Why would you now?

Alec The war. What I saw.

Dolly Are you going to tell me what you went through?

Alec No.

Dolly You will have to, if you're to get me to live in England.

Alec I can't.

> *Silence.*

Dolly Alec, tell me what you saw.

Alec Children. Dead children. Burned off the face of the earth. Millions. They saved us. The innocent. I walk through this town –

Dolly Buncrana.

Alec – that's never known a war. That's never lost its young. I hope it never does.

Dolly If we ever do, it will be our own doing.

Alec Would you do that to each other?

Dolly Alec, after what you've seen, do you not know what we're all capable of doing?

Alec She knew – Rima knew what was being done. Don't ask me how – Maybe it killed her.

Dolly No, Alec, she just died – she died happy.

Alec She died knowing Rima.

Dolly Alec, why do you want to live in England?

Alec It's my home. I need to go home. What's been inflicted on it? It's hungry. Bombed, broken, lost. England, on its knees. Poor country.

Dolly Begging for bread.

Alec Hungry.

Dolly Poor country.

Alec Lost. I have to go there.

Dolly We're going there then.

Alec Will it kill you?

Dolly You will.

Alec You can say no.

Dolly Can I? I don't think so.

Alec You might love it.

Dolly No, Alec, I won't love it. They won't love me. I'll make sure of that. That is your country. Yes, it has suffered. Yes, it's on its knees. But I am not. All right, I'll stand by you. But I'll be standing on my own two feet. And I'll be doing it for you. Not your country.

Alec (*speaks*)
I vow to thee my country, all earthly things above,
Entire and whole and perfect the service of my love.
The love that asks no questions, the love that stands
the test,
That lays upon the altar, the dearest and the best.

He sings.

The love that never falters, the love that pays the price.
The love that makes undaunted – the final sacrifice.

Dolly sings.

Dolly
And there is another country, I've heard of long ago,
Most dear to them that love her, most great to them
that know.
We may not count her armies, we may not see her king,
Her fortress is a faithful heart, her pride is suffering,
And soul by soul and silently, her shining bounds
increase,
And her ways are ways of gentleness and all her paths
are peace.

They kiss.
Esther enters the kitchen, followed by Marco and Julian.
Jamie and Anna enter from the garden.
Ned is in the garden, looking at the child in the pram.

Esther Dolly, Alec, the lamb's ready.
Justin, pour the wine.

Alec Gentleness.

Esther Anna, pass the bread.

They do so.

Alec Peace.

Esther Ned, come in.

Ned stays in the garden, looking in.

Alec Is the war over, Dolly?

Justin, Marco, Anna and Jamie raise their glasses.

Dolly I hope so.

Justin For richer or poorer – in sickness and in health – till death us do part.

Alec Is the war over?

Dolly I said I hope so.

THE BIRD SANCTUARY

For Catherine and Geraldine

The Bird Sanctuary was first performed at the Abbey Theatre, Dublin, in February 1994. The cast was as follows:

Eleanor Geraldine McEwan
Marianne Joan O'Hara
Robert John Kavanagh
Tina Maria Mcdermotroe
Stephen Risteard Cooper

Director Robin Lefevre
Designer Frank Conway
Lighting Trevor Dawson

Characters

Eleanor Henryson
a reclusive painter

Marianne Henryson
her married sister, a doctor

Robert Henryson
their brother

Tina Henryson
his wife

Stephen Henryson
their son

Setting

A house in Booterstown,
overlooking the bird sanctuary

Act One

Darkness. Music.

    *Light on a room of perfect proportions. It is apparently
in squalor.*

    *Paint stains everywhere on the floors and furniture,
and on one wall there is a whole scramble of colours.*

    There are many canvases turned to the wall.

    There is a camp bed, covered with army blankets.

    *Behind the camp bed there is a haversack with bits
and pieces of clothes.*

    *There are a small table, a small stove for heating, and
a battered armchair.*

    There are two battered hard-backed chairs.

    The table, stove and chairs are paint-spattered.

    *Scattered about the room are various pieces of a
beautiful dinner service.*

    *There are a chandelier and many candlesticks with
candles. Three paintings are visible.*

    *All in the paintings wear clothes from the 1930s and
1940s.*

    *One painting is of a woman in her thirties with a boy
resting his head on her knee, her hand stroking his hair.*

    Another is of two girls.

    *The third is of a man in his forties sitting, asleep on
an armchair, his hands folded on his lap.*

*Within this clutter there is about this room a sense of
design in its colouring.*

    *At the play's end the back wall melts to reveal the bird
sanctuary, and its colours should consist of those and
only those already seen onstage.*

*Eleanor Henryson is a woman in her fifties, utterly
unconcerned with her appearance.*

Her overalls are paint-smeared.

*There is a small streak of paint on her face and her
hands are stained grey and green.*

She is surrounded by buckets of sea water.

At her feet lie many varieties of weeds and wild flowers.

*She is examining these carefully, and continues to do
so through the opening of Act One, rejecting many
immediately, examining some more carefully and those
she may douse in the sea water.*

*From these she selects a few, placing some in a vase,
leaving others to dry on the chairs beside her.*

The vase is on the table.

*Eleanor works with utter concentration, then finding
a flower that has survived a vigorous dousing and close
investigation, she kisses it and places it in the vase.*

*The music ceases when Stephen, her nephew, enters,
carrying two buckets of sea water on a stick across his
back and in his hands a sack of more vegetation.*

*He is in his early twenties, dressed in shorts and
T-shirt, with wellington boots on his feet.*

His hair is wet.

Eleanor My little helper – you look like a Chinaman.

Stephen I feel like a Chinaman. I feel as if I've swam the
Yangtse.

Eleanor Is that in China? We must go there some day.
Wouldn't that be lovely? Sipping tea under Mount Fuji.

Stephen That's in Japan.

Eleanor Young people are so knowledgeable. Of course
I don't like rice. Do they eat potatoes there?

Stephen They eat potatoes everywhere.

Eleanor An Irishwoman in Japan eating potatoes. No, I've gone off the idea.

Stephen Of Japan?

Eleanor Of potatoes. Awful creatures. They have eyes. They look at you. Eating them now, I'll feel like a cannibal. Coincidentally, the tea you made this morning tasted like human flesh.

Stephen I've never tasted human flesh.

Eleanor Neither has your ancient aunt. I'm the oldest virgin in captivity.

Stephen Eleanor, you were never a virgin.

Eleanor I'm sure I was. Once.

Stephen What was it like, being a virgin?

Eleanor It was like a night in Cork. What do people do in Cork?

Stephen I believe they bitch for Ireland.

Eleanor Don't be arch, Stephen. You'll never get a man that way. Virility is now all the rage. That's why I'm so glad you go swimming. How was your swim?

Stephen Fine.

Eleanor You realise that beach is a health hazard.

Stephen I do.

Eleanor You can pick up anything on Booterstown Strand.

Stephen That's why I like it.

Eleanor You're so like me when I was a girl.

Stephen In manner?

Eleanor No, in dress sense. I was never out of wellington boots.

Stephen Help me out of these.

He sits in the armchair and Eleanor pulls off one of the boots.

The plane will have arrived by now.

Eleanor I do hope you've got some interesting specimens in that sack. The painting's nearly finished. Will you be glad not to have to go foraging for weeds and sea water for your funny old aunt? The neighbours will be disappointed. God knows what they imagine we're getting up to in here.

Stephen They'll be here soon, Eleanor.

Eleanor It's so inconvenient, this visit. I've so much to do. And I wish they'd insisted she'd take a taxi. Something to cost her money. She is mean, my sister, with money.

Stephen I don't remember her being mean.

Eleanor Marianne is very mean with money. They all are, doctors.

Stephen She was generous to me when I was a child.

Eleanor You are our brother's only son. The last of the name. You are a true-blooded Henryson. There would be no limit to her generosity there. But she's mean. I detest her.

Stephen More than my mother?

Eleanor I hate your mother. I detest my sister. I ignore your father. But I like you, a little. Until you turn against me. As you will, I hope.

Stephen I've so far managed to deprive you of that pleasure.

Eleanor I take no pleasure –

Stephen In fighting? You do, Eleanor.

Eleanor Have you ever smelt an old woman's fart?

Stephen Are you going to demonstrate?

Eleanor I save my finest for your mother.

Stephen Poor Mother.

Eleanor The woman's a vampire. Have you seen her teeth?

Stephen She's never forgiven you for threatening her with a crucifix.

Eleanor I knew there was a reason for having that object in the house. Anyway, she survived. Another proof for not believing in that person.

Stephen Why do you hate her?

Eleanor Pleasure, pure pleasure. How did you spring from the loins of those two? I'm quite convinced the hospital gave them the wrong baby.

Stephen No, dear Aunty Eleanor, I'm my father's son, my mother's curse, I am a Henryson. And here we all belong in Booterstown Avenue –

Eleanor In the house that overlooks the bird sanctuary.

Silence.

I will die if this house is sold. I'll stop painting. I'm sure there's plenty who would think that would be a happy death. A happy death. My mother's fervent prayer to that person. In the later stages of her illness, she stopped praying. Maria Regina Henryson. Mother. Do you ever pray, Stephen?

Stephen I did, once. It worked. I stopped then. I'm not a pushy person.

Eleanor Marianne prays. She used to pray for money. That worked too. She doesn't need to sell her share of this house. She has plenty of money.

Stephen Will my father agree to sell with her? Will they sell?

Eleanor Over my dead fanny. She'll be here soon. We'll know.

Silence.

It has a life of its own, this house.

Stephen Built in 1843 at the bottom of Booterstown Avenue, some say it is the loveliest house in Dublin, for from its windows may be viewed every watery inch, every reed and rush, all the wildness of the bird sanctuary, that is truly God's blessing on this boundary.

Eleanor No human hand should maim the creatures of the air nor build upon the silent wastes of the deep that protect all that make their habitation in that sanctuary. It is said when Queen Victoria visited Dublin, she stayed in Booterstown. Her carriage drove down the avenue and she saw this house and chanced to wonder at its beauty. At her command the carriage stopped, she walked up the path and knocked, but no one answered her. She stood there silent, looking in, still wondering who lived there and why they did not welcome her. My father said that those in livery attending her watched the great Queen's face and saw on it a shiver passing through her soul as if in sorrow for the wrongs done.

Stephen And seeing the Queen's sorrow, the woman of the house, a beautiful old woman dressed in black, opened the door. This woman said to the Queen of England –

Eleanor All sins are forgiven.

Silence.

All sins are forgiven, as my father said in his superstitious way. Utter nonsense, of course. Completely untrue. Queen Victoria visited Ireland in 1849. We moved here in 1929. I've heard of racial memory, but that fantasy is pushing it, even for this family.

Stephen I wish it were true.

Eleanor Why?

Stephen I rather fancy you as the descendant of that beautiful woman dressed in black.

Eleanor I rather fancy me as Queen Victoria. The other one is utterly batty. Rabbiting on about sin. That's the kind of old fool one sees marching down O'Connell Street parading pictures of the Pope.

Stephen I thought you fancied the Pope.

Eleanor I did find him attractive – in a Jewish sort of way. I'm an incurable romantic. Like Marianne in her own way.

Silence.

Marianne believes that story about Queen Victoria. Let her.

Stephen Yes. My father believes it too.

Eleanor Robert would believe anything.

Stephen Yes, he would. Why does Marianne believe that story?

Eleanor The workings of that woman's mind have long been a mystery to me. Three times a year we speak. My mother's anniversary, my father's, Christmas Eve. I put down the phone and I see her face. And I paint it in the bird sanctuary, my painting of the bird sanctuary – (*She begins to sob.*) Stephen, I am so nervous. I am so nervous. If they sell the house over my head – if they take away the house – for three years I've been a recluse to finish the painting of the sanctuary – Stephen – I do apologise, don't come near me – I do apologise. If that bitch Marianne starts to run down Ireland and the Irish I'll kill her. She will. She has to. Damn her.

Stephen Does she love the house?

Eleanor In her way. Yes.

Stephen Is that why she believed the Queen Victoria story?

Eleanor She believes it because my father believed it. She understood him. You shouldn't pry, Stephen, and you shouldn't bathe in that filthy sea.

Robert calls offstage.

Robert (*off*) Eleanor.

Eleanor We're back, all three of us.

Robert (*off*) We're back, all three of us.

Eleanor All in one piece, as they say.

Robert (*off*) All in one piece, as they say.

Eleanor Thanks be to God.

Tina is heard offstage.

Tina (*off*) Thanks be to God.

Eleanor I'm glad Fangs is on form.

Stephen Show some respect for my parents.

Eleanor That is choice, coming from you.

Stephen Go welcome Marianne.

Eleanor Why? She knows how to walk through the bloody door. She's been in this house often enough. I wonder what she's brought me.

> *Robert enters, carrying Marianne's suitcase and duty-free bags.*

Robert Lads, lads, lads, that sister of ours must have come like a June robin. This suitcase is light as a feather, boys. (*He kisses Stephen on the forehead.*) Marianne's looking well. Your Aunt Marianne is looking the best. At her peak. A bit pale, but we'll put the colour back in her cheeks, won't we, Eleanor? (*He kisses Eleanor on the cheek.*) She's home, Eleanor. She's looking like herself.

Eleanor What should she be looking like, an elephant? Where is she?

Robert She wanted a quick walk around the garden.

Eleanor Marianne, in a garden? That woman would cement over a window box.

> *Tina enters.*

Tina, hello. We were talking about cement.

Tina Robert, I think it's time we left for home.

Robert Eleanor meant no offence –

Tina Not her. The other one. The one we kindly picked up from the airport. The one walking in the garden. The one who's just told me to go fuck myself.

Stephen Mother!

Tina Tell that ungrateful pup I'm no longer his mother.

Eleanor Why did she tell you to have sexual intercourse with your own person?

Tina I pointed out to her there was a little chill in the morning air. I asked her if she'd like to borrow my cardigan. She said –

Robert Now that may be where you heard her wrongly. Maybe she said, Go fluff yourself. It's a fluffy sort of cardigan.

Tina I don't use the offending word myself, but I do know the sound of it, I have not completely lost my marbles, maybe she has –

Eleanor Lost her marbles –

Tina Now she may have taken offence that I had to sit in the front of the car, but I have to, I cannot sit in the back. My car sickness. Robert is my witness.

Robert Our old friend, the car sickness.

Eleanor Or she may have completely lost her marbles.

Tina Well, she was starting to cry.

Robert No, not crying exactly. More like sighs. Sobbing and saying –

Tina Ireland, Ireland, my Ireland, my Booterstown, my bird sanctuary, my home, my Ireland. Her that never had a good word to say about it or about her own.

Robert Maybe she should be fetched in, Eleanor.

Eleanor Let her look at the bird sanctuary.

Robert Tina's right, she's not looking well –

Eleanor Then why were you saying she was?

Robert I didn't want to worry your good heart.

Eleanor My good what?

Marianne enters.

Marianne.

Marianne Sister.

Eleanor My sister.

Marianne Why are you dressed like that?

Eleanor I'm still in mourning for Laura Ashley.

Marianne Why is this room looking even more like a pigsty?

Eleanor This was our parlour, dear. Don't the English believe we keep pigs in our parlour?

Marianne I dread to ask what's in these buckets.

Eleanor The Irish Sea. Ireland, Ireland, your Ireland.

Robert This is the son.

Eleanor Your Booterstown, our bird sanctuary.

Robert Our son, Stephen, you remember him.

Eleanor Your home, your Ireland.

Robert A grown man now, isn't he? Stephen, say hello to your Aunt Marianne.

Stephen Marianne.

Robert Well, the old homestead is still our own. Looking well. A bit older. Like ourselves. But you're looking the best, Marianne. I was saying to Eleanor –

Eleanor You were crying on the way here. You wanted to walk around the garden. You told Tina to fuck off. Why?

Robert I'm sure she's tired. And she left Kent early this morning. It's the flight – jet lag.

Eleanor The flight from London is one hour long. She's not tired.

Robert Hanging around in airports, the nerves about flying, it can take it out of a body, even a short flight can cause jet lag, it's dehydration. But what am I thinking of? Marianne, you'd not suffer from that. You've travelled all over the world. Australia, New Zealand, Papua New Guinea. You sent us a postcard. Isn't that a lovely name for a place? Papua New Guinea. That's where they speak Pidgin English, isn't that what you wrote to us, Marianne? And Australia at the same time. Two or three years ago. Australia. Wombats. I've always wanted to see a wombat.

Marianne Shut up, Robert.

Robert Maybe I should leave this suitcase up the stairs in Marianne's room. Tina, maybe you might make the cup of tea. Stephen, park the car somewhere else. Here, the keys.

Stephen Where is it?

Robert Just outside the front door.

Stephen Why do you want it moved?

Robert (*sotto*) I can guess what's going to happen between these two. I know who'll be blamed driving her here. I don't want my windscreen smashed. Like a good son, do as I ask you.

Stephen exits.

Robert I'll leave this lad upstairs. Tina, the kettle. (*He exits.*)

Tina A wombat. He wants to see a wombat. There's a house of yous in it. I'll make tea. (*She exits.*)

Eleanor Why are you staring at me?

Marianne To see if I know you. If I recognise you. I always knew you could be a hard bitch. Cruel. But I did give you the benefit of the doubt. I did think there was some sense of shame about you.

Eleanor You shock me. Yes, I am shocked. I did think you would be – I don't know – you would be more prepared. I admit the crying about Ireland, the walk about the garden, the love for the bird sanctuary – yes, I was intrigued. Slightly unnerved even. But you blew it. A hard bitch. Cruel. Some sense of shame. My loved sister, really! Tina may be right, you are losing your marbles. No, Tina is never right. But you are losing your memory. If I remember correctly, weren't those the same words you used when referring to my behaviour at our dear mother's death?

Marianne I know you are referring to the eighteen-piece dinner service with the red rose that my mother intended me to have after her death.

Eleanor You claimed our mother left it to you with her dying breath. Oh yes, in her agony she turned to you and she said, By the way, Marianne, do have that dinner service –

Marianne Yes, I remember –

Eleanor Her last breath –

Marianne I remember her last breath – the red rose – in her agony – shut up, Eleanor, Eleanor, shut up.

Silence.

Eleanor You may have the dinner service, if you wish it.

Marianne Thank you, I will take it with me some day.

Eleanor It might be quite difficult to pack. It's no longer eighteen pieces. It's two hundred and twenty-seven. I've broken a lot of it.

Marianne I'll still take it.

Eleanor I thought you might. Now, you mean woman, have you brought me anything from England?

Marianne I'm sure you won't like it.

She takes a black dress from the duty-free bag, Eleanor unwraps the paper from it and holds it out in her upturned hands.

Eleanor Yes, oh yes, thank you. (*She holds the dress before her body.*)

Marianne I picked it up at the last moment.

Eleanor I adore it. You perfect woman, you have taste. I don't deserve this. So expensive. You are ridiculously generous.

Marianne takes a bottle of vodka from the duty-free bag.

Marianne Are you still on vodka?

Eleanor I don't drink much. Often. (*She takes the vodka.*)

Marianne This brandy's mine.

Eleanor Naturally, unless we run out.

Marianne Now, remember that my limit is two.

Eleanor Glasses?

Marianne Bottles, for Jesus' sake, I'm still an Irishwoman. (*She hands Eleanor another bottle of brandy.*) Have you anything for me?

Eleanor Close your eyes. Keep them closed. (*She leads Marianne to a painting.*) Look.

Marianne The two of us as children. As girls. Telling each other secrets. You've given yourself a prettier frock of course. Have you anything else for me? Oh yes, this one. Our mother in her favourite dress. And that's our own little brother with his head resting on her knee, and her hand stroking his hair. Her hand. My mother's.

Eleanor Most near, most dear, most loved –

Marianne
    And most far,
    Under the window where I often found her,
    Sitting as huge as Asia, seismic with laughter,
    Gin and chicken helpless in her Irish hand,
    Irresistible . . . but most tender, most tender for
    The . . . hurt birds that surround her . . .

    Silence.

Our father, where is he? Oh yes, this one. Eleanor, he's sitting in this room. His chair, and his hands folded on his lap. Sleeping, or thinking, or watching. Father.

Eleanor They're all for you.

Marianne I don't want any, as you well know.

Eleanor OK. Then they're for sale.

Marianne I mean, I've time for you as a painter even though none of your paintings do justice to their subjects. I was a much better-looking child than you make me. And your prices are ridiculously high. They're simply not worth the money.

Eleanor Yes.

Marianne Now you're annoyed with me. Well, be annoyed. And you were always furious none of us ever went to your bloody exhibitions. Why should we go?

To be introduced as your devoted family? I mean, Jesus, people know you must have a family somewhere. Why parade them?

Eleanor You're not getting the dinner service.

Marianne Even if it were my mother's last wish?

Eleanor Particularly because it was my mother's last wish. She obviously confused you for me. It would be wrong to disobey. It would be unlucky. She wished it to stay in the family. I'm saving it as a wedding present for Stephen. The good boy is queer as a coot, but who knows, his mother's prayers may be answered. Do you know Tina blames me for it all? I think it's a new theory of the Catholic Church. What causes homosexuality? Aunts. My aunt made me a homosexual. That's all the rage in confessionals. Isn't it an extraordinary faith?

Marianne You're a witch, Eleanor.

Eleanor My mother said so. It's the way I was born. I can't help it. We were the witches of Booterstown. Come back to the coven. (*She holds her fist gently to Marianne's cheek.*) Welcome home. It will break my heart if you sell this house. Break my heart. Sell where our parents lived and died, where we were born, I cannot believe –

Marianne Shut up, Eleanor. That is not the issue. The issue is why you've let the house go to rack and ruin. Look at the state of it. And please, don't excuse yourself as the mad Irish artist, dear. I'm your sister and I'm too sensible a woman not to strangle any mad Irish artist with her bare hands.

Eleanor Something's wrong. You haven't come back to sell this house.

Marianne I left this house a long time ago.

Eleanor What is wrong?

Marianne I turned my back on this country.

Eleanor Are you going to tell me what's wrong with you?

Marianne My husband's left me.

Silence.

He's left me.

Silence.

Eleanor For a younger woman?

Marianne Yes.

Silence.

Kill her. You have the power. Witchcraft. Kill her, and you can keep this house. For life. That's why I'm here. That's the deal.

Tina enters with a teatray.

Tina Eleanor, God love you, I took a quick look into that oven of yours and I swear you'll need a shovel to clean it. I hope I'm not out of place saying this, but I've found a great new cleaner –

Eleanor Tina, you're a treasure. Thank you.

Tina There's times I don't know how to take what that sister of yours says to me. How long have we been related? Since me and Robert were courting, well over twenty-six years now. She still runs rings around me.

Marianne I'll pour the tea. Sit down, Tina.

Tina You will in your eye and you a visitor. Well, Marianne, do you see many changes in your own country?

Marianne No.

Tina There are, aren't there, Eleanor? There are. More money being made. Not much happiness, but more money. Plenty of money. Less happiness. When there was less money, people were – I don't know – people were together, together in their misery, you know. Now they're alone in their misery. Aren't they, Eleanor? This is lovely tea. Eleanor always insists on the best of everything. It's a pleasure to eat in this house. I think that's why Stephen is never out of here, he has the best of everything. You'd think his aunt was his mother. I rarely see my own son.

Eleanor You rarely see your own son, Tina, because you threw Stephen out of your house three years ago.

Tina He was old enough to be man enough to get by on his own.

Eleanor You told him never to break breath to you again.

Tina You haven't told his Aunt Marianne that, have you? You haven't told her anything, have you? That's for me to do, not you.

Eleanor She knows, Tina. Everything. About Stephen. About Robert. How he gambles everything you earn, everything –

Tina I have him on a tight rein, Marianne.

Eleanor She knows I bail you both out from my own money. She knows I couldn't have lived as a recluse without your tender care. And a car is useful, so I pay for you to keep that going on the road. She knows how terrified you are that she will sell her share of the house, because then Robert can sell his, and he will gamble the lot of it. She knows I feed and clothe you –

Tina Loans, Marianne, loans –

Eleanor Lies, Tina, lies –

Marianne Eleanor –

Tina Loans, she gives us loans, loans, Jesus, we've lost everything else, will you not leave us – leave us . . .

   Silence.

I was going to say dignity. (*She laughs lowly.*) I forgive you, Eleanor. Robert says often that you have a good heart, and I believe him. You would never leave a body stuck in bad times. No more than I would. There is an oven in there that needs cleaning. I'll do it before we leave. It's a fire hazard. I don't have my new cleaner, but nothing will replace elbow grease, will it, Marianne?

Marianne No.

Tina Would you excuse me, then?

Eleanor Of course. Thank you.

   Tina exits.

This tea is much too strong. She does indulge herself at my expense when she's let come and cook here.

Marianne How often does she come and cook here?

Eleanor When I can't be bothered, and when Stephen isn't here, then they come and eat. I allow them the dignity of maintaining a family feud. Jesus, will you not leave us our dignity, wasn't that what she said?

Marianne How bad is Robert's gambling?

Eleanor How cruel of her. My life is largely devoted to the expense of leaving them their dignity.

Marianne How much is he gambling?

Eleanor What do you wish to do this evening, Marianne?

Marianne What is he gambling at?

Eleanor I thought we might have a game of cards. Or you could go to the horse racing with Robert. Maybe the greyhounds. If that doesn't interest you, how about an evening studying the combinations and permutations of numbers that have won the National Lottery. Some weeks it's worth millions. Our brother might even instruct you in the art of numerology, or even prophecy, and the secret signs that can be given to you if you know how to read the date of the day. Our brother has a weakness. He believes in magic. My father's family believed that my mother, that wild woman from the west of Ireland, they believed she was a witch. And as Robert is the son of a witch, he believes magic will solve all his problems. That's the kind of fool he's become. He abuses the great gift. So maybe you too should avoid his excessive belief in the art of magic and we'll settle down tonight to a simple game of cards. Not poker, too many fights. Let's play something less dangerous. Strip Jack Naked? Snap? Happy Families?

Marianne It was always on the cards that you would turn against –

Eleanor This happy family?

Marianne Yes.

Eleanor My God, Marianne is going to cry. Don't tell Daddy or we're all in trouble. Not that I blame you. Do you see the state of us? Do you see what you've come home to? It takes its toll. This house. This family.

Marianne You've been living as a recluse for three years –

Eleanor I have to.

Marianne Why?

Eleanor I'm painting the bird sanctuary. If I don't, it will be lost, and I can't afford any distractions from my work.

Marianne How will it be lost?

Eleanor The sanctuary? There will come a time when Booterstown will be under the sea. It's global warming. It's a scientific fact. The water will rise and flood everything. And the beach is already ruined. Sewage, pollution. I have to remember and record it. This is happening in my lifetime. Jesus Christ, the idiots were even threatening to build a road through the sanctuary. A road through one of the country's pride and joys! The country's gone mad. Can you blame me for turning into a recluse?

Marianne This country was always mad. Always. That will never change. So mad nobody notices it any more. Now, where am I sleeping? Here, or Robert's?

Eleanor In your own room.

Marianne Is it in squalor as well?

Eleanor It is better to live in squalor than to live in hate.

Marianne Are you referring to my marriage?

Eleanor You hate him.

Marianne I married him, and I will save my marriage.

Eleanor Why?

Marianne If I don't, our mother will kill me.

Eleanor Our mother's dead.

Silence.

Marianne Our mother will kill, you know that.

Silence.

Eleanor I can find my way about the squalor.

Marianne And I about the hate.

Eleanor It's what I know, what I take my strength from.

Marianne Yes. Can you get him back?

Eleanor Who is she?

Marianne An Australian. We met her there a few years ago. In Tasmania.

Eleanor He's left you for a Tasmanian?

Marianne She's very beautiful. Very healthy.

Eleanor Any other irritations?

Marianne She's improving her mind. It's to impress his friends. I've been reliably informed she was seen reading Tolstoy on a train.

Eleanor A Tasmanian reading Tolstoy on a train. How alliterative. I will try to grant you your wish.

Marianne kisses Eleanor.

Marianne You do have a kind heart.

Eleanor So I am told, but have yet to believe. I have been kind enough to clean your bedroom. But I am sure it is not yet sufficiently beautiful for my loved sister's demands. There is more to do. Tina will be delighted to help me. Excuse me, loved one. I do know you need time to talk to the house alone. I'll leave you to its whispers. (*She exits.*)

Marianne Well, dear house, have I asked too much this time? Do you finally have my measure? One should always be prepared. I thought this time I was. She sees through me. She catches me out. You help her. Well done.

Robert and Stephen enter.

Robert Has the storm settled? Is the coast clear? Where's herself? Are we safe?

Marianne Eleanor's cleaning my bedroom.

Robert Eleanor never cleans up after her. Tina must be doing it.

Marianne Tina's gassing herself in the kitchen.

Robert She couldn't be. It's not New Year's Eve. She threatens that. The Christmas is a rough time for her, the last few years, you know yourself. Anyway, less said the better. I say, take to the bed, pet, you take to the bed and pretend it's not the time of year that's in it. It's sent to afflict people, Christmas. New Year. And I find I can laugh her out of it eventually. And a good laugh clears the air. Lifts the spirit, as they say. As long as she can laugh she'll be grand. She can still do that, for in her own way, she's a gas ticket. Do you remember how I could make you laugh when I was a boy? Once Eleanor shut herself up in her world, you daren't enter, but Marianne, no matter how hard she was studying her medicine, she had time, you know, she took the time. Mammy wasn't at her best after I was born, and Daddy was Daddy, but Marianne was a gas ticket, me and your aunt had some laughs. We could say anything to each other. And we still could, couldn't we?

Marianne In our way, yes.

Robert Gas tickets. Look, say nothing, but I'm popping out to Blackrock to see a man about a horse. Numbers two, three, seven is where the luck lies today. The problem is what race will the combination show up in. Do you want me to lay the few pounds on for you?

Marianne Is it a certainty? (*She gives him money.*)

295

Robert Right, now say nothing. Stevie, if anything is asked, I'm out for cigarettes. Say that like a good son. I won't be five minutes. (*He exits.*)

Marianne A gas ticket, your father.

Stephen Yes. Wouldn't he break your heart?

Marianne Fathers do.

Stephen It seems to be their destiny.

Marianne Yes. Robert seems to have taken your decision well.

Stephen My decision? I suppose you're right. I'm in good health. And you?

Marianne Excellent. And Eleanor?

Stephen As my loved father would say, the best, the peak, the wonder of the world, my sister, a good heart, the best.

Marianne She's Eleanor. No, she's not. Not quite the same old sixpence. I'm worried, Stephen. She's sometimes slightly out of control. Does she ever leave the house?

Stephen No.

Marianne What's she doing?

Stephen Painting.

Marianne Is she getting an exhibition together?

Stephen Just one painting.

Marianne The bird sanctuary?

Stephen The house, the bird sanctuary, and the sea beyond it.

Marianne One bloody painting in three years, apart from the family album? Is it enormous? It will never sell.

Stephen She's selling the old stuff. It's selling everywhere.
She's making a fortune. They go for a lot of money.

Marianne How could she do this? I trust she takes no
pride in it. I was expecting them as my inheritance. My
inheritance from her. She'll die before me. She's much
older.

Stephen She's not that much older, my dear.

Marianne She is considerably older, young man.

Stephen Four years –

Marianne More like ten years – don't look at me like
that. I think four years is considerably older. She's
frightened of dying, Eleanor is, you know. Terribly
frightened. Beyond her control, that. Death. So am I.
That's why she never liked me. She wanted rid of me.
When I was born, the day I was born, she came to me
with a bar of chocolate. I took it, my father said, but
I didn't eat it. She's never forgiven me for not choking on
that chocolate. She wants me out of sight, out of mind.
She encouraged me to emigrate to England. She knew it
would kill my father. It did. He never forgave me for
marrying an Englishman. He wanted us to be a credit to
Ireland. To Dublin. He trained us to speak as we do.
Do you not know, he used to argue, that the best speakers
of the English language, are well-educated Dubliners. But
Daddy, we sound like the English, Eleanor would argue,
and he would say, you are Irish and you can outdo the
English, that is our revenge. You must love the English
language, and we must speak it beautifully. And so we
tried to do, to please our father. That has certainly
helped me in England. There are many times, many,
many times I pass as an Englishwoman, and this helps
me in my practice in Kent. Kent was the orchard of
England, we were told at school. When I went there

as a young bride I thought Kent would smell of apples. It didn't. It smelt of England, the rest of England. I worked so hard to fit in. And to make our practice work. I saw patients any time of day and night, I did the books, I did the social round. I did the hard slog. He – my husband – called me the Irish navvy. This was his idea of a compliment. Or else in front of our English friends he would call me the Irish maid, the Irish skivvy. We would be serving drinks before dinner, and if someone needed more ice or tonic, he'd say, ask the Irish maid. All these years I've tried to fit in and through thick and thin I've made wonderful friends, but I didn't really belong there, although in general I loved the people. And the older I get, the more I'm aware I did not belong there, yes. And I've wasted my life married there, working my fingers to the bone.

Stephen If you hadn't gone, would you have wasted your life here?

Marianne I would have ended up like Eleanor. I wouldn't have married. Certainly not to an Irishman.

Stephen Why not an Irishman?

Marianne I have no lesbian tendencies. So, if I hadn't married, I could well have wasted my life. All in all, it seems fair to say that it was my destiny to waste my life. I should be grateful to realise that at least. Are you in love?

Stephen Yes.

Marianne Fool.

Stephen You haven't asked me who with?

Marianne I have no desire to pry.

Stephen You should. I'm having an affair with your husband. He visits Ireland secretly. I insist we stay in

the finest suite of the Shelbourne Hotel. We make love.
I humiliate him each time. I make him do as he doesn't
wish to. He obeys me. Then I call him my English maid.
My English skivvy. And if he does not obey, if he is not
my English maid, then he will not know the strength of
his Irish navvy.

Marianne How very kind you are, Stephen. You have
lifted my heart. An excellent twist to the tale. Eleanor
has trained you well. But this is all your own work. My
sincerest congratulations. A stranger might have believed
every word.

Stephen That's because they're strangers.

Marianne And we are loyal. Eleanor places such a high
value on loyalty. She loses nearly everyone through that
insistence on loyalty. No one can meet her demands.

Stephen Yes, they can.

Marianne I do believe you can. But what good will it
do us? You're no more going to fill the earth with little
Henrysons than Eleanor did. You're the last of the line.

Stephen We'll put up a fight.

Marianne We always do.

Stephen We sometimes do.

Marianne Yes.

   Tina enters.

Tina Where's Robert gone to?

Stephen He's gone for cigarettes.

Tina I was asking you, Marianne.

Marianne Stephen's just told you, for God's sake.

Tina I heard no one, I saw no one.

Stephen Hear no evil, see no evil.

Tina Evil.

Marianne How long has this lunacy being going on?

Tina As long as it needed to. Rather, as long as it will need to, until he comes to his senses. Your room is ready, Marianne. Go up and see the lovely job we've made of it. When you look at the state of this kip you're standing in, you'll find it a wonder two such rooms could be in the one house.

Robert enters.

Where were you?

Robert Getting a few odds and ends for Marianne. And some cigarettes for myself. In Blackrock.

Tina You took the car to Blackrock to get a packet of cigarettes?

Robert The weather was lovely, so I thought I'd drive. Marianne, will I ever forget the weather the time we were in Kent? Wasn't it roasting? How is Kent? I thought it was one of the most beautiful places in the world. The villages we drove through. They were like doll's houses. Like the towns in Stephen's story books when he was a boy. And the people, so kind, in Kent. The men, so handsome, and all the women spoke like the Queen. But sure this one, Marianne, work, work, rush, rush – we barely saw her.

Tina (*sotto*) I wonder why.

Robert What, Tina?

Tina It was lovely, Kent. England. Lovely.

Robert Do you remember it, Stephen?

Stephen Yes, Maidstone and Ashford, was it?

Tina That's in Ireland, Ashford. Hunter's Hotel. The best food in Ireland.

Stephen They had jousting competitions somewhere in Kent.

Tina I ate spinach there one night Eleanor brought us. She had a woman from Finland staying with her. A beautiful creature, another painter. The spinach was like velvet.

Marianne Will you eat out with me tonight?

Robert It was a happy time. Kent and Hunter's Hotel. The best. Years ago. Sad. Time passing.

Marianne Will you be my guests at dinner tonight? Book a restaurant –

Robert Herself – Eleanor – she doesn't – as you know – go out. No point in giving offence. Very kind to ask. Lovely gesture, Marianne. We can't –

Marianne Where is she?

Tina She's made her getaway. You've had your quota of time from her. She's upstairs painting. Every room in the house is full of the painting. Bar your own, of course, and we'd to clear out a whole load of stuff to have it spick and span for yourself –

Marianne I'm asking you out for a bite to eat –

Robert Have you ever wondered if a body could eat a seagull? What would they taste like? Rotten, I'd say. When I was driving to Blackrock, I saw a school of them on the shore, and I said to myself, If the worst came to the worst and you were depending on those boys for your meat, what would be on them? Not much, not much. Mind you, what the same lads dine on themselves, I'd say you'd need a hole in the stomach to get one down you. Aye, seagulls, they're the boys. Smarter than you might think. Smarter than hens. Poor old hens, scratching a living, minding their own business, laying an egg or two, happy and innocent as the day's long, and in the end, the twisted neck, the legs in the air, and there they are, in the oven. Still, there's nothing like the bit of chicken. But ours is not to reason why. Hens. Seagulls.

Marianne I would like to bring us out tonight, the whole family.

Tina I thought you were informed we were no longer a family.

Robert Who spoke about that?

Tina Your sister.

Robert Marianne, pay no attention to that. It's nonsense. Stephen is a chip off the old block. He's like myself. Until the right girl slips by, he'll keep his hand on his penny. Won't you, boy?

Silence.

The right girl, like myself. Me and Tina. Tell me, Marianne, am I not the lucky man?

Marianne Yes, you are, Robert.

Tina I'm glad somebody's lucky.

Robert Do you hear her? Do you hear that mother of yours, Stephen? Could you be up to her?

Stephen Yes, I could.

Robert Isn't the weather lovely today? There's nowhere like Ireland if you get the good weather. Marianne, do you remember Mrs Centra, the beautiful old Italian woman who ran the chip shop in Blackrock – long gone now –

Tina That chipper's turned into a shaving accessories shop. What is Blackrock coming to? You can get fifty different types of men's perfume, but try buying a pound of onions and they look at you as if you're mad. Mad.

Robert Anyway, I was saying about this Italian woman, she used to sit there shivering, dressed in black after the husband died –

Tina I mean, a pound of onion isn't much to ask for.

Robert Tina, you hate onions. What are you complaining about?

Tina I am not complaining. I am merely pointing out –

Marianne The Italian woman, Mrs Centra, used to say – (*She mimics an Italian accent.*) Ireland – Irlanda – could be loveliest country in world, but rain – rain – rain.

Robert That's it, she remembers. Rain – rain – rain.

Tina What's the point of this story?

Robert What's the point of buying onions if they disagree with you?

Tina Shut up, Robert.

Eleanor enters.

Robert Don't you tell me to shut up.

Eleanor Home, home on the range. Am I hearing a discouraging word?

Marianne You took your time upstairs.

Eleanor Yes, I was sitting in our bedroom. I've not spent much time there recently.

Marianne I take it you live mostly in this room?

Eleanor Yes, my studio.

Marianne Our sitting room. And I've not spent much time here either, but I do remember a beautiful room, elegantly furnished, the centrepiece of one of Dublin's loveliest houses. Queen Victoria admired it. And now, well, Tina called it a kip. I can't better that description. It's filthy, it smells, it is disorderly –

Eleanor If there was ever order in this room, that was because it served the purpose of the family who lived in it.

Marianne Our family.

Eleanor There is still order in this room, because it serves my purpose, for I live here. It is still a beautiful room, and it is my studio. My studio. I will do what I please, I will paint where I wish to. I will live in it as I desire and I decide. I live here. Let that be an end to it.

Marianne Let that be no end to it, big lady. I will not see this house turn into a tenement. We were each left this house, and I will have it cleaned completely and I will have you out of it if I have to haul you out of it with my bare hands.

Eleanor Fuck off, you red-nosed bastard.

Marianne I am not a red-nosed bastard.

Robert Girls, girls, girls.

Tina Very nice, very ladylike.

Marianne You're the red-nosed bastard.

Eleanor You are not selling this house.

Marianne I am selling my share of this house.

Eleanor You are not –

Marianne And Robert is selling his share.

> *Silence.*

Eleanor Robert?

> *Silence.*

I see. A little conspiracy. Two against one. I'm not surprised. Always the same.

Marianne We decided together.

Eleanor Robert?

Marianne He won't change his mind.

Robert Eleanor, you know yourself how hard things have been. We haven't a penny. We need the money.

Eleanor Tina?

> *Silence.*

You know he'll spend it in six months.

Tina It's his to spend.

Robert It's not like that, Eleanor. I'll invest it.

Eleanor Jesus, where did we find you, Robert? Do what you like. But remember, two against one. You pair of skunks.

Robert It's for the best, Eleanor. You'll let it fall about your ears.

Eleanor Then sell it. Sell the house.

Robert Eleanor, we are sick worrying about you. You have to go and face the world again. Stop burying yourself in here.

Eleanor Dear house, we will soon be making our farewell to you. We have lived long in your service. Perhaps we have grown tired of that service, or you have grown tired of us. What are you? Bricks and mortar, slate and wood. Windows. Is that all? Without you, what will happen to me? Without me, you'll survive. How will you remember me? A silly, old woman who one day, late in the evening, three years ago, decided to do something decisive with her life.

Tina Eleanor, please.

Eleanor I walked through the open door and went into the water to clean myself of past and present. Late in the evening it was, when the beach at Booterstown is deserted, but this evening, it wasn't. There was another woman walking alone. It was my sister by marriage.

Tina Eleanor, for God's sake.

Eleanor She saved me from the sea, waded in after me and hauled me out with her bare hands. She said, Eleanor, it's me, Tina, for my sake don't do this. Don't drown yourself. If you die, how will I live? She said, how will I live? I looked at her. I let her walk me out of the ocean. She should have let me die.

Tina Is that why you hate me?

Eleanor In this family, hate, like love, is only a figure of speech. But that day I felt I'd made a decision. And now, this day, a decision is made for me. A momentous day. And I will not fight the decision, I will celebrate it. In this family on momentous days we have a feast. And this night a feast we will have. In this house. I want to have a feast. Tina, can you organise that?

Tina After what you've just told –

Eleanor For God's sake, woman, you'll recover from that. You cope marvellously.

Tina There's very little time to organise –

Eleanor Then move now. Get to the shops. Chickens, salads, cheese, the usual. Charge it to my account. Robert, you must help her shop and cook. And remember, chicken. Wings, legs, bones. I need the bones.

Tina You're making a stock?

Eleanor Yes. Hurry, I've work to do.

Robert I'm glad you're taking it so well, Eleanor. You're some soldier. Sad. But you're a brick.

Eleanor Thank you, Robert. I've always wanted to be a sad brick.

Tina Eight o'clock –

Eleanor Perfect, we'll see you then. Goodbye. And Robert? Drive carefully.

Robert What? Do you hear her? The evil eye, she's putting it on me. Listen to her. The woman's a brick.

Eleanor And I wish I were going through your windscreen.

Robert Listen to her.

Eleanor Sad. Goodbye.

Robert Right. We're off. Come on.

Tina Eight o'clock then. All hands.

Robert and Tina exit.

Marianne May I ask what that whole performance was in aid of? It came without warning.

Eleanor That suicide attempt was quite genuine.

Marianne You didn't let me know. Why didn't you phone?

Eleanor I didn't want to worry you excessively.

Marianne I suppose you were put into some kind of home?

Eleanor No, I made a miraculous recovery.

Marianne Good, I'm glad you pulled yourself together.

Eleanor Thank you, Mother Teresa.

Marianne I met her in Calcutta. She's a beautifully logical woman with no time for shilly-shallying. She's an excellent nurse. Anyway, I wasn't referring to your ridiculous suicide. Drowning, how could you? Witches can float. I'm talking about your ludicrous reaction to my threat to sell the house. You know our deal.

Eleanor I know it, you know it, and it is imperative Robert knows nothing about it. A good move to let him think you're both in cahoots. I will be plagued by him for life if I bring this off.

Stephen Bring what off?

Eleanor I told you earlier not to pry, young man. Live and learn. Here are your two poor lonely aunts, sitting lost in their later years, asking for nothing more than a little light refreshment, and here we are left to languish. What has become of the younger generation?

Stephen A bottle of chardonnay?

Eleanor Please.

Stephen exits.

I do wish Stephen would play soccer. He has the arse for it.

Marianne When did you get interested in soccer?

Eleanor The last World Cup. Ireland did terribly well. We didn't win any matches, but we drew with absolutely everybody. For a violent country it set a wonderful example. Such a good time. The whole nation was joyous.

Marianne I knew nothing about it.

Eleanor No, you wouldn't.

Marianne How will you kill her?

Eleanor Music, my little one?

Stephen enters with the wine and serves.

Schubert?

Marianne Yes, please.

Eleanor Darling, I've some work to do. Excuse me if I continue. I'll decline a drink while I'm working. Stephen, entertain Marianne. Play her the Schubert.

She hands him the cassette, which he plays.

Marianne How will you kill her?

Eleanor Reads Tolstoy, you say?

Marianne Yes.

Eleanor I see. No rest for the wicked. (*She works.*) A meal with the family, a painting to finish, and a little accident to arrange. You'll be the death of me, Marianne. What a night we'll have of it. Is the chardonnay gorgeous?

Marianne Perfectly chilled, yes.

Eleanor Good health, dear sister.

Marianne Good health.

Music. Fade.

Act Two

Night.

  Candles are lit.

  There are the remains of a meal and empty bottles of wine.

  The room itself has been cleared of a large part of its objects.

  Eleanor is alone, dressed impeccably in black.

  She sips wine and gently dismembers a chicken carcass.

  She holds up a bone and kisses it.

Eleanor Blue. (*She produces a blue thread and winds it around the bone.*) Blue, the colour of hope, a thread of blue. (*She holds up another bone, pours some of her wine on it.*) Black. (*She produces a black thread and winds it around the second bone.*) Black, the colour of poverty, of charity, a thread of black. Bread to break, the food of faith. (*She breaks bread over the bones.*) Wine to drench these bones in blood. (*She pours wine over the bones.*) It is done. (*She slants the bones into the shape of a cross, tying them together with white thread.*) May her hands and feet be pierced, may they number all her bones. This night may she be received into her reward of paradise. (*She bows her head.*) I'd have made a wonderful Catholic priest. Maybe that's why I fancied the Pope. Anyway, that's Miss Tasmania on her way.

  A door slams.

Good God, who is that? Who have I raised? I hope I haven't surpassed myself. Perhaps it's the devil.

Tina (*off*) It's me. Tina.

Eleanor No, just the usual horror. Dear old Dracula.
I can handle her.

Tina enters.

Tina I'm on my own.

Eleanor I thought you might have been accompanied by
the devil.

Tina I'm in the company of the devil.

Eleanor You're cross with me, I could tell over dinner.
Why?

Tina You well know why. Forget your smart answers
for once, I'm in no mood to give you a chance to use
them. You excelled yourself earlier today. This is my first
opportunity to have it out with you. That talk about
me saving you. Jesus, Eleanor, can you keep nothing to
yourself? I should drag you to the shore now and drown
you myself. But I'm contented with giving off to you to
your face, so I won't. I'm back to do a bit of cleaning up
stuff here. The rest are still in Gleeson's pub.

Eleanor Did any of the barmen ask for me?

Tina Not one mentioned your name.

Eleanor How quickly they forget you in pubs when
you're not spending money.

Tina You spend enough on carry-outs if the number of
bottles were gathered. And forgive me for saying this
about my own sister-in-law, but for a doctor, Marianne
can knock back a fair few brandies.

Eleanor They all can, doctors. It's something to do with
their hormones. Like acne.

Tina Doctors get acne?

Eleanor Yes, haven't you noticed? They get younger every year. I suppose by the time we die they seem like children. Dangerous children at our deathbed.

Tina Stop talking about deathbeds and dying. It's not lucky.

Eleanor You'll never die, Tina.

Tina We all do.

Eleanor Vampires don't.

Tina I thought we had agreed you would stop calling me that name. What the hell is this? (*In the process of cleaning up, Tina has found the tied bones.*)

Eleanor Don't touch that. It's not lucky.

Tina What is it?

Eleanor It's a charm.

Tina What kind of charm?

Eleanor To kill someone.

Tina drops the bones.

Tina You've put the heart sideways in me. What's this kind of talk? In the name of Jesus –

Eleanor He's already been called upon.

Tina You have invoked the holy name –

Eleanor Not quite, I made indirect reference to him. It's metaphor. You should try it sometime, dear. Metaphor. It's very good for the vocabulary.

Tina Eleanor, you're mad, the mad woman of Booterstown, mad –

Eleanor I'm the nice woman of Booterstown, I don't trouble anyone.

Tina You've just said you're trying to kill somebody.

Eleanor It's nobody we know, Tina.

Tina Then who is it? Why are you doing it?

Eleanor For Marianne. She's asked me to.

Tina Why?

Eleanor You met her husband?

Tina Him? Yes, years ago.

Eleanor And what did you think?

Tina He was very nice.

Silence.

Eleanor What did you think of him?

Tina He had the airs and graces of a duchess and the manners of a pig. The one time we visited them, he kept us under lock and key in case anyone should see us. He insulted Robert, he called Stephen a sissy, and he treated her, Marianne, like dirt. She should have left him years ago, but he is a handsome man, and she's cracked about him. Don't listen to her, Eleanor. This is a fight between husband and wife. Don't interfere. Don't kill him.

Eleanor He's leaving her.

Tina Who for?

Eleanor A younger woman.

Tina Slice her head off.

Eleanor touches the bones.

Eleanor I plan to.

Tina I'll drink to you on that. Good woman. (*She fills their glasses.*) Good health.

Eleanor Good health.

They drink. Silence.

Tina Stephen.

Eleanor Why Stephen?

Tina Is he any good as a painter?

Eleanor He's my assistant. He does his own work in his own room. I never look at it. He never asks me to. When and if he's any good, he'll show me it. I doubt if that will happen while he is living in my house, because if I find out his work is good, I'll put a match to it.

Tina You're more cruel than I am.

Eleanor I do speak to him. You don't.

Tina There's nothing to say.

Silence.

Good health.

Silence.

You should not have said today what you did say. You had no right to tell what you told. You have every right to talk about yourself and what you did, about what you were going to do to yourself. I don't think it came as a surprise to any of them. I'd told Robert. He phoned Marianne. She said, Do nothing. As Robert always does. Nothing. But you had no right to tell them what I said to you. That I would die without you. It wasn't you I said that to. In the panic I was saying it to Robert. When I pulled you from the water, I saw you as Robert, because I – I just imagined you were Robert.

Eleanor Why?

Tina Your father – he did it, didn't he, after your mother died? Don't lie that it was an accident. I know everything. I married one of this breed. I married Robert. Some nights he thinks I'm sleeping, he starts to walk through the whole house. And he keeps on walking. There's the rare time he sits on Stephen's empty bed and I hear him crying. When he finally comes back to our bed, I still let on I'm asleep and I put my arm out so that it's around him, and he lies there, not sleeping. I know there's something not right. So I imagined you were Robert, and I said to you, I'll die without you.

Eleanor Would you?

Tina Die? Without him? No, I wouldn't, no. I loved the man I married. Didn't I go into his mad family? I knew they'd look down their noses at me because I had neither brains nor breeding. You did, you all did – you especially. Well, I took your abuse and I handled it well, and do you know why? Your own mother had the abuse of your father's family, she survived it, she even thrived on it. Now I didn't thrive on it, the cruel words cut me to the quick, the insults, but Robert didn't insult me, and I cherished him, so I cherished his mother and father, his sisters, for he loved you all. And as I've said, the man I married I loved. And we had a son. The joy, his joy, all your joy. No more. No longer. And Robert is also no longer the man I married. He is no longer the man – no longer.

Eleanor pours Tina a glass of wine.

It is not easy to be a vampire, you know. You get no sleep at night. And the price of blood, it's shocking.

Eleanor Shocking.

Tina Eleanor, say something smart to put me in my place.

Eleanor I would have died without you.

Tina Hence, you hate me.

Eleanor Don't let them put me on the street. Don't evict me. Don't let them sell the house.

Tina Jesus, you're frightened.

Eleanor From the day she was born, Marianne has frightened me. She is a woman who always gets what she wants. Do you know, there's times I feel sorry for that handsome brute of an Englishman she married? Once, he was quite kind. Full of energy. Talent. She got her claws into him when they were young, and turned him into a husband and father. She took his passion and made it hers. He became staid and solid and silent. I understand it. It's the terrible attraction of the Irish for the English, and the English for the Irish. Together, they behave as expected. She's mad, he's cruel, that's the way. They should never have married, but they are. And it's gone on so long, they're set in their ways. Secure. Christ, I'm glad there's still sufficient life left in him to leave her.

Tina Will he?

Eleanor raises the bones.

Eleanor She is family. She is my sister. We marry for life when we marry.

Tina I see.

Eleanor I'm glad you do. I owe you one, Tina. I'd hate to see anything awful happen to you.

The door slams shut and there is a roar of singing 'With Catlike Tread'.

317

Tina They're drunk as skunks.

> *Tina fills their glasses.*
> *Marianne, Robert and Stephen enter, still singing.*
> *Marianne is dressed in elegant black.*
> *Robert and Stephen are wearing dinner suits.*
> *Stephen has loosened his bow tie.*
> *Robert wears a heavy black overcoat, which he keeps on for a short while.*

Robert It's ourselves, women.

Eleanor It is indeed, good brother. In loud voice.

Marianne The best.

Robert We heard a great one over across. In the pub. Marianne, you were the happy woman, laughing. Tell it to them.

Marianne I'll never remember it all.

Robert You will.

Marianne You tell it.

Robert We'll help you out. There's this boy walking up Leeson Street on a Friday night, and he's got a car key in his hand. He's just walking up and down Leeson Street, looking at the key. He is paralytic drunk and this policeman comes up and says –

Marianne Excuse me, sir, what are you doing?

Robert So your man says, My car, my car, where is my car? It was at the end of this little key, now it's gone. Where is my car?

Marianne Am I right, Robert? The policeman looks down and sees that your man's prick is hanging out of his trousers. So he points and says, Excuse me, sir, but your dick, your manhood, your penis –

Robert What about it? I'm looking for my car. It was at the end of this little key. Where is my car?

Marianne Your dick is sticking out, the policeman says. So your man looks down and sees the prick and he says –

Robert My wife, my wife, where is my wife?

Robert and Marianne fall into each other's arms, laughing.

Tina And where was his unfortunate wife?

Robert What?

Tina I suppose it was the unfortunate wife who had to send a policeman after her drunken sot of a husband? I trust to God she got her own car keys and drove home safely herself. She likely had a house of children to care about. Let him bare his ding-dong to the nation.

Marianne That's given us all something to think about. I trust Robert, and you, Stephen, that you will never bare your ding-dongs to the nation. Not that a bare ding-dong would do much for me. I've seen too many.

Tina Yes, but you were a doctor in England, so it's mostly Englishmen's. It's a well-known fact that the Irish are, you know, more – more than the English.

Eleanor More what, dear?

Tina Why settle for a radish when you can have a turnip?

Robert Now, Tina pet, a turnip –

Tina All I'm saying is that the Irish are better equipped in the fireman's hose department.

Marianne How do you know this?

Tina They have more children.

Marianne I had three children by an Englishman, you had one by an Irishman.

Tina As a general rule, the Irish have more children –

Marianne That's because the Bishop of Rome forbids them to –

Tina I know what he forbids and he is quite right. I would just like to say that I would let no man touch me with a plastic bag strapped to his cock.

Stephen I know what you mean, but in the dangerous times we live in –

Tina Shut your perverted mouth.

Silence.

I don't like the course this conversation is taking.

Eleanor You took it on that course.

Tina I did not start attacking Irishmen, I did not start attacking the Catholic Church. She did. And I would also like to add that I'm amazed she had three children by her husband. I'm amazed he didn't abort them.

Marianne You dirty rag you.

Eleanor Do you know I'm one of the few Irishwomen to admit in public that I've had an abortion. That, and a miscarriage.

Marianne You never had either.

Eleanor That's true.

Marianne Then why admit it?

Eleanor It gave one something to say at dreadful dinner parties. I was usually drunk and tearful, and it did provoke other people into making the most revealing confessions.

Stephen Such as who?

Eleanor Such as you. But I can't recall many of the others. Remember, I was drunk and tearful. I think that's where I got the reputation for being kind-hearted. I listened to it all and nodded wisely.

Stephen I believed you when you told me that.

Eleanor I believed you when you told me you were gay.

Stephen I am gay.

Eleanor Good, then you're one up on me, aren't you?

Robert has been looking at the dismembered chicken.

Robert We made short work of this chicken.

Eleanor We did indeed.

Marianne Why did you think I would abort my children?

Tina Not you – him. Your husband.

Marianne Good Christ, no. That's one thing he wouldn't have done. He loved having children. Maybe he wanted more. Maybe he'll have more.

Robert Now, Marianne, put that out of your head. You're not to come back here with a babby in your arms. You'll give Tina ideas.

Tina Will you put a plastic bag on it?

Robert Maybe you'd fancy another one, Tina?

Tina God is good, his ways not ours to work out, but at my age, not even he could work that miracle. Besides, I had one child. It was ample.

Stephen Thank you.

Tina I repeat, I *had* one child.

Marianne You still have.

Tina No.

Stephen No. No indeed. (*He pours himself more wine.*)

Robert Families fight. All families fight.

Tina No, not all. Just the ones hell-bent on destroying each other.

Marianne Our parents didn't fight.

Robert No, they didn't.

Tina They were perfect, I presume.

Eleanor Quite.

Tina Then what happened to yous three?

Eleanor We lost them, I suppose.

  Silence.

Do you still hear their voices?

Marianne Every day.

Robert Clear as a bell.

Stephen What do they say to you?

Eleanor We are not yet drunken and tearful.

Marianne Eleanor?

Eleanor What?

Marianne Will we go out for a walk? Down to the beach? Down to see the bird sanctuary?

Eleanor It's the dead of night.

Marianne I want to walk through it. I want to see the sanctuary in the night.

Eleanor You can see it through the window.

Marianne
Through the window – thro' a mirror clear
That hangs before her all the year,
Shadows of the world appear.
There she sees the highway near . . .
    The Lady of Shalott.

That's what you've turned into. The Lady of Shalott.

Eleanor The Lady of Shalott was suffering from pre-menstrual tension, and I am past childbearing.

Marianne 'I am half sick of shadows,' said The Lady of Shalott.

Eleanor You are half sick with brandy, Marianne.

Marianne Yes, I must slow down. I must stop drinking. I did once.

Eleanor For how long?

Marianne Twenty minutes. It was savage. A New Year's Day. My husband took me aside and pointed out I hadn't been sober since Christmas Eve. It was a gross exaggeration. He then hinted a little too heavily that I might have a drink problem. I disagreed and went out and smashed his car windows. That cured him. I'm a peaceful woman, but a drink problem was asking for it. May I have a little mineral water? (*She pours herself some.*)

Eleanor Would you like a little something in it?

Marianne Don't be bitchy, Eleanor. It suits you.

Stephen May I have some as well?

Marianne hands him the bottle of mineral water.

Tina I'm glad somebody's slowing down. He learned to drink in this house, not his own.

Robert We never have drink in our house.

Tina Of course we don't. If we did, you'd drink it. He had Stephen on the beer by the age of fourteen.

Eleanor We were taught to drink by the age of ten.

Marianne No, he didn't trust you on it, Daddy, but he did trust me. He was determined that from the earliest age I would appreciate a good vintage.

Eleanor Marianne, Daddy would have drank his own urine.

Marianne Yes, he would have, poor darling. He probably didn't want to drink alone.

Tina So he started you on the bottle at the age of ten?

Marianne He did. He had his own little ways.

Robert I was frightened to drink in front of him.

Marianne Why?

Robert I was frightened of him.

Silence.

He thought I was stupid.

Silence.

I mean, very stupid. Very, very stupid.

Silence.

Not fit to be his son. The doctor's son. I wish he'd seen Stephen grow into a man. Lived to see him. Daddy could have coped well with all this. I mean, put sense into him.

The way I can't. I do try, he himself will tell you that,
but I can't. You know yourself. Yes, very, very stupid.
Those were his words, Daddy's, when I failed the Leaving
Certificate. You may think I am disappointed in you,
Robert, but I am not, he said, because you are and
always will be stupid, very, very stupid. I am content
that you can at least write your name, he said, but I am
sad that it is our family name. Henryson. You have failed
me, he said, but I am not disappointed. I stood in his
surgery looking at him for a good hour. I knew he
wanted me to leave, but I didn't want to. And I didn't
say a word back to him. Do you know, from that day
I've been tongue-tied. He frightened me. He wouldn't
have wanted to see me drunk. Not in front of him.
I didn't want to let him down. I still hear him, every
day, clear as a bell.

Tina The more fool you for listening. More fool all of
you.

Robert Sell the house. Be rid of it. Please.

Silence.

In our own ways it's left us all in the state we're in.

Eleanor Which is?

Robert Unhappy.

Eleanor Speak for your damned self, Robert.

Marianne You've insulted our father.

Robert No.

Eleanor We've heard you.

Marianne He's heard you.

Robert He hasn't.

Eleanor He'll punish you.

Robert He won't. Stop it, stop it.

Marianne Then apologise.

Eleanor Apologise now. Say you're sorry in front of him.
Say it now.

She hauls him before the portrait of their father.

Robert I am very sorry.

Eleanor You dared to bring any of this up in public?

Marianne You dared to say this in front of strangers?

Tina His own wife? His own son? Strangers?

Robert I apologise. I am sorry.

Marianne You've spoken to your father, now speak as
him to your son.

Robert No.

Marianne Then you have failed.

Robert Yes.

Stephen What has he to say to me, my grandfather?

Tina Stephen, do not get into that world.

Stephen What has he to say to me?

Eleanor Abort, miscarry.

Stephen As you have?

Eleanor As I pretended, and you believed.

Stephen Yes.

Eleanor What great faith you have, Stephen, may you
keep it.

Stephen And you.

Eleanor I will. Keep the faith. In this family. That it will live for ever. That's what I want to pretend. My great strength. It's allowed me to lock myself away and work and work until it's finished, the bird sanctuary, and I will paint it, for the family, and when it's finished, I may lose the faith, I may stop pretending, but I wouldn't bank on it.

Stephen Will it be worth it?

Eleanor The painting? Good God, no. Who cares about a bird sanctuary? About a family house in Booterstown? A family so fucked up by its fear of death that it's ceased in some way to live. It's all a waste of time and effort, this painting, my dear, but it is all I know how to do, so I will continue believing.

Marianne Oh Eleanor, shut up and have a glass of wine. Why don't you finish it tonight and put yourself out of your misery? You'll never sell the damned thing, that's for sure, it's too big to fit in anywhere. And if you die before I do, as you will, I will certainly not cart it across the Irish Sea. So finish it and burn it. Then do some nice landscapes of the west of Ireland. They're quite pretty, and they sell.

Eleanor Will someone plug that woman's mouth with her second bottle of brandy?

Marianne I haven't finished my first.

Eleanor No, but I have. Hard cheese.

Tina It can't be lucky painting a bird sanctuary. Birds are not lucky in a house. I would never tolerate even the idea of a budgie. Dirty, nasty little creatures, letting on they can sing. Sing my arse. Who ever heard worse than that chirping? I mean, would you listen to a record of a budgie?

Marianne Some people listen to the accordion, some people even play it. I myself would prefer to throttle a budgie, but there's no accounting for taste in music.

Tina I have taste in music. My mother had a fine voice.

Stephen starts to hum the chorus from 'After the Ball Was Over'.

Stephen
　　Many's the heart that's aching, if you could read
　　　　them all,
　　Many's the fond hope that's vanished after the ball.

Tina (*sings lowly*)
　　Though lights were shining in the big ballroom,
　　Softly the organ was playing a tune,
　　There stood my sweetheart, my love, my own,
　　I wished some water, leaving the room.
　　When I returned, pet, there stood a man,
　　Kissing my sweetheart as lovers can.
　　Down went the glass, pet, broke in the fall,
　　Just like my heart was after the ball.

Tina and Stephen sing together.

Chorus
　　After the ball is over, just at the break of dawn,
　　After the dance is ended and all the stars are gone,
　　Many's the heart that's aching if you could read
　　　　them all
　　Many's the fond hope that's vanished after the ball.

Silence.

Tina (*sings*)
　　She tried to tell me, tried to explain,
　　I would not listen, pleading in vain –

Silence. Tina sings.

I broke a heart then after the ball.
I broke a heart then after the ball.

Silence.

My mother's song.

Marianne As I said, there's no accounting for taste in music.

Tina It can't be lucky painting a bird sanctuary.

Stephen pours Tina a glass of wine, which he leaves before her.

Birds are unlucky. They say.

Marianne God, she's going to give us a blast of 'My Singing Bird'. (*She fakes a soprano accent and sings.*)

But there is no one can sing as sweet,
My singing bird, as thee,
Ah-ah-ah, ah-ah-ah, my singing bird as thee.

Eleanor Thank you, dear. Thank you, both. That is enough. We do not need these delightful memories of our native shore. We are not miles from the land where our true lover sleeps. We are not in exile from Ireland.

Marianne I am, usually.

Eleanor You chose to be in exile.

Marianne I married an Englishman, for Jesus' sake.

Eleanor You got pregnant by an Englishman.

Marianne It was more than you ever did.

Eleanor I didn't want a child. I would have preferred a budgie.

Marianne Which brings us back to where we started. Which is always the same in this house. Nothing ever changes here. Is it any wonder you're as demented as you are? Why don't you drink yourselves to death? At least that would bring a change. If one of us died, would that not at least be a sign that the rest of us are alive? Why doesn't one of us die? Why don't we do something and die?

Tina If a bird flies into your house, get rid of it. Even if it's a robin, which got its red breast from the blood of Jesus on the Cross, flying close to him, trying to give him solace with its song.

Marianne I do believe Old Mother Riley is about to give us a folk cure –

Tina There's no cure for it.

Marianne For what?

Tina A broken heart.

Marianne There's no cure for lung cancer, there's a cure for broken hearts.

Tina For Aids. There's no cure for Aids.

Marianne There will be.

Tina When?

Silence.

Marianne Soon enough. Even as things stand, with the advance in drug research and the more we know, you'd be amazed –

Tina Not for the people who died from it. There's no cure for the people who died from it.

Stephen Ma, you're in dangerous territory.

Tina I'm in the bird sanctuary, or as near next to it as makes no difference. And I never liked birds. They're unlucky. Big black birds. That's what it is. Aids. Big black birds. There was a film on the television over the Christmas. The birds started to attack human beings. They went for them. They wanted to kill them. They broke a small girl's glasses. They were pecking out her eyes. These birds. And what had started them attacking? It wasn't explained in the film. Maybe it was cruelty, human cruelty. I have been a cruel woman.

Stephen No.

Robert Enough.

Tina I turned my back on my young.

Stephen There was two of us in it. Stubborn, the two of us.

Robert The two of yous, I said enough.

Tina I am unlucky.

Stephen Stupid, the two of us.

Tina I have brought you bad luck, Stephen.

Robert Will you shut up? Will you shut up now? There is nothing wrong with Stephen. He does not have that disease. My father is too good a doctor to let us die from any disease, and you've inherited his brains. He would save us from death –

Marianne He's dead, Robert, our father's dead.

Robert Marianne.

Silence.

No.

Marianne They found him on the beach. He drowned in shallow water. Some whispered he took his own life, but I'd say he had an attack, a slight stroke out walking, or his heart maybe, a broken heart after Mammy died. No cure for that, yes? If you want my professional opinion, I'd say that's what happened, and he died, I pronounce him dead. My dead father. Still impossible to believe. I know. Freud did get one thing seriously wrong. At least in this family. We don't want our fathers to die. We want them to live for ever. They don't. That's our secret. We want them to live for ever. And we can never tell them that secret, can we, Stephen? My loved Robert, your son does not have Aids. That is correct, isn't it, Stephen? I'm not your doctor, but I am your aunt, and I'd say he is safe. He is so like Eleanor. Too clever to give too much to outsiders, and too independent to take anything, or anyone, too seriously. They will always have the cruelty of the virgin. Don't mistake me. The same Eleanor has screwed up more men and more women than any of us will ever be told. But when it comes to the crunch, when push comes to shove, all she's ever given birth to is her own imaginings, so she's never given herself –

Eleanor I've given myself to each and every one of you.

Marianne What a waste of giving. What a waste of a fuck. Don't be shocked at that expression. Every mother, if the truth were told, has said it about her child at some time or other. But forgive me, I forget you wouldn't know that.

Eleanor I wondered how long it would take for the marvels of having three lovely children to be paraded in front of me.

Marianne You've never forgiven me for having children.

Eleanor On the contrary, I was delighted you were fertile in that respect, because in every other respect you are a barren old bitch.

Marianne Robert, you heard what she said to me.

Robert Drink talking, drink talking, drink.

Marianne It's always the same.

Robert Let it pass, Marianne, pet. Ignore her.

Marianne She is a witch.

Marianne runs to Robert for comfort.

Tina Have you noticed, son, when you start talking about your own bother to these three, they change the subject to their own?

Stephen I have.

Marianne She was always jealous.

Robert Best of families, fights –

Marianne We're selling the house over her head.

Robert If that's what you want –

Marianne I'm going to burn her bloody paintings.

Robert You might burn down the house, then what will we sell?

Marianne You're so sensible, Robert.

Tina Stephen, if I ever turn into one of them, have me put down.

Stephen All right.

Marianne Look at her, sitting there sipping drink, my brandy, wearing the dress I bought her, and the face on her. There's not an ounce of sorrow in her.

Robert Now I'm sure she'll say she's sorry.

Eleanor laughs.

Tina Will you walk me home, son? I'm not driving.

Stephen Will I be let into the house?

Marianne My mother was right to disown her on her deathbed.

Robert She didn't, Marianne. That's not true.

Tina hands Stephen a key.

Tina I had the locks changed, but I got a key cut for you.

Marianne My mother did disown her. She did. She called her the devil's child. She used to do it all the time. A changeling, she called her. A crazy woman. She's not my sister.

Eleanor
'Fair and foul are near of kin,
And fair needs foul,' I cried.

Tina But please, son, no men in your bed. The shock I got before.

Marianne Witch. Give me back my brandy. And my house.

Tina I'm not up to it. Well, at least, no men from Cork.

The phone rings.

Eleanor It's for Marianne, unless I'm mistaken. Calm down and answer the phone, my loved one.

Marianne How do you know it's for me?

Eleanor You've been expecting news from England, haven't you? Answer the phone. Now.

Marianne Hello, yes, yes, it's me, what's wrong? You're weeping, what . . . My good God . . . My good God . . . Are you alone? Are the children with you? . . . Of course I will. First flight tomorrow . . . My darling, how terrible . . . I know. I love you, thank you . . . Thank you, I'm with you . . . All sins are forgiven. You know that. All sins are forgiven. (*She replaces the receiver.*) A family friend in England. She's dead. A young Australian. Well, Tasmanian actually.

Tina She's crocked it?

Eleanor Tina, show some sympathy. Poor Marianne is in a state of shock. My sister, you need a brandy.

Marianne Please, a large one.

Eleanor How did she die, this unfortunate Tasmanian?

Marianne She was travelling back to Kent on the last train. It was absolutely jammed. She was standing in the corridor reading a book. Absolutely immersed in it, my husband says.

Eleanor Which book, dear?

Marianne *Anna Karenina.*

Eleanor Tolstoy. And Anna dies in an awful train accident.

Marianne She must have leaned against the door and just beyond Bromley she fell off the train.

Eleanor I never cease to marvel at the power of the Russian novel.

Marianne chokes on her brandy.

My dear, you are quite overcome with grief. Tina, help me with her. Robert, Stephen, leave us. This is something only a woman's heart can feel. Well, a woman of a certain age.

Marianne What do you mean, a certain age?

Eleanor Be quiet, Marianne. Move, men, leave us.

Robert and Stephen leave.

Marianne The house is yours for life.

Eleanor Thank you. My own one, stop thinking about me. What about you? I know how music charms the savage breast of grief. Would you like me to play a little something?

Marianne Is it the Hallelujah Chorus from Handel's *Messiah*?

Eleanor Yes.

Marianne Please do.

Eleanor plays the music. The women raise their glasses to each other. Marianne embraces Eleanor. Tina shakes their hands. The women raise their glasses again. Robert enters.

Robert Why are you playing that music? There's been a death.

Eleanor switches off the music.

Eleanor She went a little mad with grief. She wanted to hear it. You may both come back in now.

Stephen enters.

Robert Are you all right, Marianne?

Tina She's as right as she'll ever be, aren't you, girl?

Marianne You're all terribly kind to me. It was such a shock.

Robert Do you remember the last time we played that music?

Eleanor Indeed I do. Summer, 1990. The World Cup. Ireland against Romania.

Marianne What happened?

Robert She doesn't know what happened, my own sister? We won. A penalty shoot-out. Great game, but the nerves. It all came down to the last penalty, and who took it but O'Leary. David O'Leary.

Eleanor He'd never taken a penalty before.

Marianne How do you know that?

Eleanor Everybody knows that.

Marianne Eleanor, you wouldn't know a penalty if it hit you in the mouth.

Eleanor It didn't hit me in the mouth and it didn't hit the Romanian either. He scored, O'Leary. We won. Ireland won. The joy of the whole country.

Robert Every art and part.

Marianne What happened next?

Eleanor We played Italy.

Marianne And we lost. I watched that.

Robert So you did know –

Marianne That we failed? Yes.

Robert The Italians won, but we went out singing.

Marianne Jesus, give me a gun.

Robert Let no one say we can't take a beating.

Stephen It was very quiet that night though, Dublin.

Tina Yes, very quiet.

Robert You could have heard a pin drop in Booterstown Avenue.

Marianne Because we failed?

Robert To win? Yes, we did. We failed.

Silence.

Marianne Failed. Yes. My father wanted me to stay in Ireland. I didn't. He wanted Eleanor to be an architect. Jesus. All of us, we let him down, didn't we?

Eleanor Some considered him a failure because he married our mother. A doctor and a servant girl from the wild west of Ireland. But I don't believe they failed. We were each conceived in happiness, and if time has taken its toll on happiness, then to hell with it.

Marianne Hell and happiness.

Tina Hell or Connaught, Cromwell told the Irish, go to hell or to Connaught. Well, now he's in hell, Cromwell, and we're not in Connaught. Fuck him.

Marianne She's lying there in Connaught. My mother, in Sligo. He lies beside her, my father. That was his wish. Stephen Henryson and his wife, Maria Regina.

Stephen I know their story.

Eleanor Which one?

Stephen The only one.

Marianne Then tell it to us.

Stephen The man was asked one day, Do you, Stephen, take this woman, Maria Regina, to be your lawful wedded wife? To have and to hold –

Tina In sickness and in health –

Robert For richer and for poorer –

Marianne In comfort and in sorrow –

Stephen Till death do you part? He said, I do. So do I, said the woman, take this man to be my lawful wedded husband. Soon the woman said, I am with child. And they called her Eleanor, after her father's mother. The woman said, I am again with child, and they called her Marianne, for Saint Anne is the patron saint of mothers, and Maria is her own mother's name. The woman said, I am with child, and they called him Robert, the name of both their fathers, and he was both their son. They lived and died in Booterstown Avenue, blessed by the grace of God.

Eleanor I wish I believed in that, but I don't.

Marianne The grace of God? Yes.

Robert Indeed.

Eleanor They did.

Marianne Yes.

Tina Yes, and isn't it strange that Protestants can't dance? Mind you, they have beautiful skin. Mine is like a bush. I blame the Famine.

Robert (*sings*)
Salve, regina, mater misericordiae,
Vita, dulcedo, et spes nostra, salve.
Ad te clamamus, exoules filii Evae,
Ad te suspiramus, gementes et flentes
In hac lacrimarum valle.
Eje ergo, advocata nostra, illos tuos
Misericordis oculos ad nos converte.
Et Jesum, benedictum fructum ventris tui,
Nobis, post hoc exsilium, ostende.
O clemens, o pia, o dolcis virgo Maria.

Silence. Stephen is asleep, his head resting on Tina's knee, her hand on his hair. Robert has closed his eyes, his hands folded on his lap.

Eleanor They're dead to the world.

Marianne It's the dead of night.

Eleanor You'll go home tomorrow?

Marianne I will. He needs me.

Silence.

Thank you.

Eleanor You asked. You received. As always.

Marianne Thank you. Shall we tell each other secrets?

Eleanor If you like.

Marianne Yes.

They sit together.

Did you try to drown yourself?

Eleanor Yes.

Marianne What for?

Eleanor I was lonely.

Marianne We're all bloody lonely, dear.

Eleanor Yes.

Marianne Will you do it again?

Silence.

It's a rush always, isn't it? My coming and leaving here.

Eleanor It is.

Marianne Would you like me to stay? Would you like me to live here?

Eleanor Sometimes. When I want a walk. When I want to go out.

Marianne Will you go outside again?

Eleanor Tomorrow I will. I promise you.

Marianne How can I believe you?

Eleanor I'll go to the airport with you.

Marianne Why?

Eleanor To say goodbye. The painting's finished, by the way.

Marianne When?

Eleanor Close your eyes.

Marianne Closed.

Eleanor Can you see my signature?

Marianne Eleanor Henryson.

Eleanor That's it. That's the proof I did it. Proof I exist, Eleanor, daughter of Stephen and Maria Henryson, who lived in a house on Booterstown Avenue, overlooking the bird sanctuary. How do you hear their voices, Mammy and Daddy's?

Marianne Built in 1843, some call it the loveliest house in Dublin. Queen Victoria remarked on it. From its windows –

Eleanor – may be viewed every reed and rush, all the wildness of all who live in this house.

Marianne Where all sins are forgiven.

Eleanor Where all sins are committed.

Marianne No human hand should maim the creatures of the air nor build upon the silences of the deep that make their habitation in this sanctuary.

Eleanor I have locked myself away to seek that sanctuary. And dear sister, I wish to show you why. For once, keep your silence. This is, as I've said, proof I have existed, proof we have lived in Booterstown Avenue. You have travelled the earth, to Asia, to Australia. This night let your carriage drive down our avenue. You see this house, walk up the path and enter. A woman answers you, for she saw a shiver pass through your soul. And seeing this sorrow, the woman, dressed in black, opens the doors, shows you her room, points to the walls and lets one melt, so that you may be granted your wish, you shall walk with me into eternity, into the bird sanctuary that is waiting outside. It is as simple as stepping outside, Marianne. Don't, until I tell you.

The back wall magically reveals the bird sanctuary.

If you look, you'll see it. The bird sanctuary. Believe me, you'll see it. Pretend, pretend. Keep the faith, dear sister.

Marianne I do, Eleanor.

Eleanor So do I, Marianne.